TITLE OF LIBERTY

by

Ezra Taft Benson

Mark A. Benson, Compiler

Published by
DESERET BOOK COMPANY
Salt Lake City, Utah
1964

Printed by

DESERET NEWS PRESS

in the United States of America

Republished by

Archive Publishers

754 East 50 North
Heber City, UT 84032

435-654-0824
www.archivepublishers.com

2011

Dedication

To the ever-increasing number of
modern-day patriots who are rais-
ing the Title of Liberty throughout the land.

EZRA TAFT BENSON

Preface

A true spokesman for liberty, Ezra Taft Benson will be remembered by liberty-loving Americans as one of the great patriots of our time.

Here is a man who has never feared being controversial in defense of freedom and liberty. As he, himself, declared, there are too many of us who "stumble around in the middle of the road trying to avoid 'controversy' and get hit by traffic going both ways."

Ezra Taft Benson will always be controversial if it means speaking out against the socialistic state; warning us of the very real threat of communism; urging us to develop anew true patriotism; challenging us to stand fast by our God-inspired Constitution; and imploring us to defend America as "a land choice above all other lands."

As he has continued to speak forthrightly on these vital issues of our day, numerous requests have come to compile these addresses into a single volume. Many of these addresses were delivered in the latter part of 1963, prior to Elder Benson's call to preside over the European Missions of The Church of Jesus Christ of Latter-day Saints.

Readers of this volume will find Ezra Taft Benson's voice a clear and strong one—a warning voice to all Americans. Through a lifetime of church and government service he has seen the liberties we all cherish erode away from the onslaught of creeping socialism and godless communism. Yet, he has a deep and abiding faith in the American people—that if we are "alerted and informed" we will rise to the challenge and not sell our birthright for a mess of socialistic and communistic pottage.

Thus the timeliness of *Title of Liberty*.

My special thanks go to Alva H. Parry of Deseret Book

Company who has been of particular assistance throughout the preparation of this book.

Finally, my deep appreciation to my father for allowing me the opportunity of compiling his addresses and for the blessing and privilege of having a father who has never been afraid to stand up and be counted on the side of freedom and liberty.

MARK A. BENSON

Publisher's Foreword

Deseret Book Company has experienced genuine satisfaction in the publication of this provocative book, *Title of Liberty*, by Elder Ezra Taft Benson of the Council of the Twelve, currently serving as President of the European Missions.

In days of uncertainty, doubt, and fear the clear-cut message of such courageous, vigorous challenge brings hope in place of despair. The book is needed and noteworthy. It sounds a message of encouragement, based on the determination of those who read to set their goals in tune with truth and to maintain them.

It is with a sincere desire to perpetuate the ideals of freedom and free agency that Deseret Book Company presents this thoughtful and stimulating volume, *Title of Liberty.*

THE PUBLISHER

Contents

. . . Moroni rent his coat; and he took a piece thereof, and wrote upon it—In memory of our God, our religion, and freedom, and our peace, our wives, and our children—and he fastened it upon the end of a pole.

. . . he called it the *title of liberty* . . . and he prayed mightily unto his God for the blessings of liberty to rest upon his brethren, so long as there should a band of Christians remain to possess the land—

—Alma 46:12-13. (Italics added.)

"Let Us Live to Keep Men Free"

Humbly and gratefully I stand before you—grateful for patriots such as you—humbled by the magnitude of the task before us.

I am here tonight with the knowledge and consent of a great spiritual leader and patriot, the President of The Church of Jesus Christ of Latter-day Saints, President David O. McKay.

As an introduction to my remarks and a fitting tribute to our honored guest Robert Welch I quote the following from Edmund Burke:

"How often has public calamity been arrested on the very brink of ruin, by the seasonable energy of a single man? . . . I am as sure as I am of my being, that one vigorous mind without office, without situation, without public functions of any kind, (at a time when the want of such a thing is felt, as I am sure it is) I say, one such man, confiding in the aid of God, and full of just reliance in his own fortitude, vigor, enterprise, and perseverance, would first draw to him some few like himself, and then, that multitudes, hardly thought to be in existence would appear and troop about him."

I speak to you as a fellow citizen of the United States of America deeply concerned about the welfare of our beloved country.

I am not here to tickle your ears—to entertain you. I will talk to you frankly and honestly. The message I bring is not a happy one, but it is the truth, and time is always on the side of truth. "Truth must be repeated again and again because error is constantly being preached round about." (Goethe, 1749-1832 quoted in the *Freeman,* July, 1958.)

I realize that the bearer of bad news is always unpopular. As a people we love sweetness and light—especially sweetness. Ralph Waldo Emerson said that every mind must make a choice between truth and repose. Those who will learn nothing from history are condemned to repeat it. This we are doing in the Americas today.

George Washington stated, "Truth will ultimately prevail where there are pains taken to bring it to light." To bring the truth to light is our challenge.

Lincoln said, "If danger ever reaches us it must spring up amongst us; it cannot come from abroad. If destruction be our lot, we must ourselves be its author and finisher. As a nation of free men, we must live through all time or die by suicide." Our real problem is internal—here at home.

Today we are in the midst of continuing international crisis. The outlook for world peace and security is dark indeed. The gravity of the world situation is increasing almost daily.

The days ahead are sobering and challenging.

All over the world the light of freedom is being diminished. Across whole continents of the earth, freedom is being totally obliterated.

Never in recorded history has any movement spread its power so far and so fast as has socialistic communism in the last three decades. The facts are not pleasant to review. Communist leaders are jubilant with their success. They are driving freedom back on almost every front.

It is time, therefore, that every American become alerted and informed about the aims, tactics, and schemes of socialism and communism which are essentially a war against God and the plan of salvation, which is based on freedom of choice.

The fight against godless communism is a very real part of every man's duty. It is the fight against slavery, immorality, atheism, terrorism, cruelty, barbarism, deceit, and the destruction of human life through a kind of tyranny unsurpassed by anything in human history. Here is a struggle against the evil, satanical priestcraft of Lucifer.

Yes, the days ahead are sobering and challenging.

Three years ago a beloved spiritual leader delivered an inspiring prayer at the dedication of a temple near London, England. I quote a short paragraph from that memorable prayer:

"Next to life, we express gratitude for the gift of free agency. When Thou didst create man, Thou placed within him part of Thine Omnipotence and bade him choose for himself. Liberty and conscience thus became a sacred part of human nature. Freedom not only to think but to speak and act, is a God-given privilege." (President David O. McKay.)

"Can the liberties of a nation be thought secure when we have removed their only firm basis, a conviction in the minds of the people that these liberties are of the gift of God? That they are not to be violated but with His wrath?" (Thomas Jefferson, *Works* 8:404.)

Our heritage of freedom is as precious as life itself. It is truly a God-given gift to man. Since the time of the council in heaven—and it is my faith we were all there—the fight of liberty-loving people for freedom has continued.

Free agency is an eternal principle vouchsafed to us in the perfect law of liberty—the gospel of Jesus Christ. Freedom of choice is more to be treasured than any earthly possession. As a United States citizen I believe it is guaranteed in our heaven-inspired Constitution. Yes, freedom is an inherited, inalienable, divine gift to men.

When the Savior of mankind wished to impress on his hearers the fruits of his teachings, he used these words: ". . . the truth shall make you free." (John 8:32.)

We are moral agents with freedom to choose between right and wrong.

Past material advances have been the fruit of our freedom—our free enterprise capitalistic system—our American way of life—our God-given freedom of choice.

Progress of the future must stem from this same basic freedom.

Because our forefathers—yours and mine—fought for the ideal of freedom; because our fathers preserved that ideal through our free competitive enterprise system under our God-given free agency; because they were willing to make religion the vital force of daily living, all of us have climbed through the years to new heights of well-being and inner strength.

But it is not only in the moral choice of right and wrong that man is free. Among the relentless quests of human history is the quest for political freedom. When the American patriot, Patrick Henry, shouted his immortal, "Give me liberty or give me death," he did not speak idly. When at Philadelphia in 1776 the signers of the Declaration of Independence affixed their signatures to that sacred document, they, in a very real sense were choosing liberty or death. Not one of them but knew full well that if the revolution failed, if the fight for freedom should come to naught, they would be branded as rebels and hanged as traitors.

The inspired founding fathers formulated a system of government with checks and balances protecting the freedom of the people. But even this was not enough. The first order of the new Congress was to draw up a Bill of Rights—ten amendments guaranteeing for all time the fundamental freedoms that the American people insist are theirs by the will of God, not by the will of government.

Yes, the founders of our country bequeathed to us a heritage of freedom and unity that is our most priceless political possession.

But to be enjoyed, freedom must be won continually.

It is high time we realized the dangerous threat of creeping socialism and its ruthless comrade, atheistic communism. When socialism is understood, we will realize that many programs advocated, and some of those already adopted in the United States, fall clearly within the category of socialism. What is socialism? It is simply governmental ownership and management of the essential means for the production and distribution of goods.

For thirty years we have aided the cause of the atheistic-socialistic conspiracy by permitting socialists, communists, and fellow-travelers in high places in government; by giving away vital military secrets; by squandering much of our material resources; by recklessly spending ourselves to near bankruptcy; by weakening our free enterprise system through adoption of socialistic policies; by wastefully bungling our foreign affairs; by ever increasing confiscatory taxation and by permitting the insidious infiltration of socialistic communist agents and sympathizers into almost every segment of American life.

Our freedoms were not achieved, and they cannot be maintained by simple short-cuts that attempt to bypass basic economic principles. These economic laws are immutable just as much so as the moral laws, the laws of nature, or the Ten Commandments.

The paramount issue today is liberty against state slavery. Both communism and socialism would destroy our economic system and replace it with socialism.

"In dealing with the treacherous Red Kremlin and its satellites, the road of appeasement is not the road to peace. It is surrender on the installment plan." (J. Edgar Hoover, American Legion Convention, Miami Beach, Florida, October 18, 1960.)

Some timid, vacillating political leaders proclaim that communism is something we will have to learn to live with ... whether it is Khrushchev, or some other leader. Peaceful co-existence they gullibly call it. The present communist system, they declare, will continue because there is no alternate system to replace communism. The policy of increasing power, of pushing their system outward and using the Communist Party they say, will go on.

Such a negative attitude writes off the hundreds of millions behind the iron curtain as a lost cause. Surely no courageous, liberty-loving citizen will treat the communist secret combination as "Something we will have to learn to live with."

There is a more courageous and sounder point of view. I say to you: "Men will be free. There is no freedom under socialistic communism. . . . Sooner or later the people will rise against it. They cannot oppose the fundamentals of civilization and of God. They can't crush their people always. Men will be free." (President David O. McKay.)

Daniel Webster has said:

"If the true spark of religious and civil liberty be kindled, it will burn. Human agency cannot extinguish it. Like the earth's central fire, it may be smothered for a time, but at some time or other, in some place or other, the volcano will break out and flame up to heaven."

There are those who recommend that the clash between communism and freedom be avoided through disarmament agreements. Abolishing our military strength and adopting an unenforceable contract as a substitute to protect us would go down in history as the greatest mistake free men could make in a time of peril.

Thank God for a great, courageous, patriotic organization which has taken "the position that it is both immoral and stupid to enter into any treaty with criminals who have no respect for treaties.

"The communists say that promises, like pie crusts, are made to be broken; that they enter into treaties only for advantages to themselves, and with no expectation of abiding by such treaties. And they have proved by their actions, in violating dozens of solemn treaties before the ink was hardly dry, that they are just as unscrupulous as they claim to be.

"Amid the infinite confusion around us today, the only safeguard is the moral standard. The important question about any proposed action, by a man or by a nation, is not

'Is it smart?' but 'Is it right?' Entering into the test-ban treaty with the Soviet murderers is morally wrong. And for that very reason it is assuredly unwise." (John Birch Society Press release Sept. 1963.)

That statement has the ring of statesmanship not vacillating weakness which today imperils freedom.

I concur with President McKay when he said:

". . . I would not deal with a nation which treats another as Russia has treated America. It is a condition which cannot be permitted to exist." (*Church News*, August 6, 1952, p. 2.)

President McKay also declared:

"Force rules in the world today; consequently, our government must keep armies abroad, build navies and air squadrons, create atom bombs to protect itself from the threatened aggression of a nation which seems to listen to no other appeal than compulsion." (*Gospel Ideals*, p. 304.)

This statesman-like declaration parallels the historic statement by George Washington when he vigorously warned:

"There is a rank due the United States among nations that will be totally lost by the reputation of weakness. If we would avoid insult, we must be able to repel it; if we would secure the peace, it must be known that we are at all times ready for war."

The conspiracy to weaken the United States involves attacks on many fronts. To weaken the American free-enterprise economy which outproduced both its enemies and allies during World War II is a high priority target of the communist leaders. Their press and other propaganda media are therefore constantly selling the principles of centralized or federal control of farms, railroads, electric power, schools, steel, maritime shipping, and many other aspects of the economy—but always in the name of public welfare.

The paramount issue today is liberty against state slavery. It is in this spirit that President McKay stated:

"Communism is antagonistic to the American way of life. Its avowed purpose is to destroy belief in God and free enterprise. . . . The fostering of full economic freedom lies at the base of our liberties. Only in perpetuating economic freedom can our social, political and religious liberties be preserved." (Excerpt from Inaugural Address for Dr. Henry A. Dixon, President of U.S.U. delivered by President McKay at the U.S.U. Fieldhouse, Logan, Utah, 3-8-54.)

It is significant to me that 120 years ago the Prophet Joseph Smith after attending lectures on socialism, made this official entry in Church history: "I said I did not believe the doctrine." (*History of the Church*, Vol. 6, p. 33.)

No true Latter-day Saint and no true American can be a socialist or a communist or support programs leading in that direction. These evil philosophies are incompatible with Americanism and the true gospel of Jesus Christ.

In the Old Testament we read: "My people are destroyed for lack of knowledge: . . ." (Hosea 4:6.)

As in Old Testament days we need knowledge today. We need to know our enemies. We must assess clearly and accurately the perils that face the free world as we enter the missile age.

The power of communism depends to a large extent on public ignorance. Knowledge is a dangerous thing—to totalitarian states; but knowledge is strength to a free people.

Internationally, communism seeks to isolate us from the rest of the free world. Here at home, communism ceaselessly pursues the disintegration of the American way of life. It strives to use education, science, literature, art, even the churches, to undermine our free society.

I was delighted to see recently the committee for the

Monroe Doctrine reprint excerpts from the famous memorandum on the Monroe Doctrine written by President J. Reuben Clark, Jr. For years I served with this noble man in the governing councils of the Mormon Church before his recent passing. As early as September 1923, he warned us at a religious service in the Salt Lake Tabernacle about certain communistic trends which have now transpired. Later in 1949 he stated:

"The paths we are following, if we move forward thereon, will inevitably lead us to socialism or communism, and these two are as like as two peas in a pod in their ultimate effect upon our liberties. . . .

"We may first observe that communism and socialism —which we shall hereafter group together and dub Statism—cannot live with Christianity, nor with any religion that postulates a Creator such as the Declaration of Independence recognizes. The slaves of Statism must know no power, no authority, no source of blessing, no God, but the State. The State must be supreme in everything. . . . For if men are free in belief about God, they will finally assert their God-bestowed rights, and this would be fatal to Statism. So under Statism God must go, and with Him goes freedom of conscience and of religion, the first two of our liberties named in our Bill of Rights. . . ." (J. Reuben Clark, Jr., *Church News* September 9, 1949.)

Recently the Supreme Court handed down another one of their tragic decisions which brought forth the comment from President McKay that the court is leading this country down the road to atheism.

The only threat to the liberty and independence of the American people from abroad is the threat of world communism spreading from its base in the Soviet Union.

But the best authorities are confident that the Soviets will not provoke a major war. Their economy would not support it.

Lenin said, "The soundest strategy in war is to postpone operations until the moral disintegration of the enemy renders the mortal blow possible and easy."

Commenting on Lenin's statement the Indianapolis *Star* adds: "Where then does the real danger lie? It lies with us—the American people.

"Other great civilizations have died by suicide. The first free people, the Greeks, died thus.

"And why did Greece fall: 'A slackness and softness finally came over them to their ruin. In the end more than they wanted freedom they wanted security, a comfortable life, and they lost all—security, comfort and freedom.'

"It is the same with Americans today. The danger that threatens us is an internal danger. . . .

"It is our own ignorance—ignorance of our own history and our heritage of liberty that threatens us. . . . Our lack of faith in freedom and ourselves, our own lack of confidence in the greatness of America and all that she stands for morally and materially is what puts us in mortal danger.

"Too many of us are afraid—afraid of atomic war, afraid of the disapproval of our allies or the neutrals, afraid of the threats and boasts of the bloated tyrants in the Kremlin, afraid to offend others by taking action to defend ourselves."

We must never forget that nations may—and usually do—sow the seeds of their own destruction while enjoying unprecedented prosperity.

If we lose our freedom, it will be because we did not care enough—because we were not alert enough—because we were too apathetic to take note while the precious waters of our God-given freedom slipped—drop by drop—down the drain.

Heaven forbid that this should come to pass!

Let us remember that we are a prosperous people today because of a free enterprise system founded on spiritual, not material values alone. It is founded on freedom of choice— free agency—an eternal God-given principle.

The founding fathers, inspired though they were, did not invent the priceless blessing of individual freedom and respect for the dignity of man.

No, that priceless gift to mankind sprang from the God of heaven and not from government. Yes, the founding fathers welded together the safeguards as best they could, but freedom must be continually won to be enjoyed. We must never forget these facts.

This is America—the land of opportunity! A land choice above all other lands! Let us keep it so!

My own political and economic creed is a simple one. I commend it to you:

I am for freedom and against slavery in any form.

I am for social progress and against socialism.

I am for a dynamic economy and against waste.

I am for the private competitive market and against government intervention.

I am for private ownership and against governmental ownership and control of the means of production and distribution.

I am for national security and against appeasement and capitulation to an obvious enemy. May I comment on this last item.

Just a short time ago Fidel Castro broadcast to the world his boastful confession that he had been a hard-core communist all of his adult life. He gloried in the fact that he had been able to confuse and deceive many people simply by saying he was not a communist. And because there were people in this and other countries who believed his false assertions, he was able to establish a Soviet beachhead only ninety miles from our shores. Americans must face the cold hard fact that Fidel Castro was encouraged and supported in his seizure of Cuba. Why? Simply because many Americans were led to believe the falsehood that he would resist Soviet influence and restore the basic freedom of the

Cuban people. Others were consciously aiding the conspiracy.

A few of us, including Robert Welch, issued early warnings based on unimpeachable evidence. Two United States Ambassadors repeatedly warned that Castro was part of the communist camp and that he was working for the communist conquest of Cuba. These voices went unheeded.

This is merely a repetition of the same deceitful pattern which was used after World War II to have us tolerate revolutionary communists in China, to accept them as so-called "agrarian reformers" and allow them to seize and enslave some 450,000,000 people on the Chinese mainland.

This is the same deceitful pattern which we have been asked to accept in the Congo, in Laos, in British Guiana, etc. In fact, everywhere the communist conspiratorial machinery is preparing for a seizure of power, we are assured there is no immediate danger from communism. We are told that the high political officials in these countries, who surround themselves with known communist advisers are merely trying to reconcile the various political factions and make their governments more representative. Later, after each country is taken over by the Fidel Castros, we are then assured that these men "betrayed the revolution." Research subsequently reveals that these men had been hard-core communists for many years. Those who believed them, once more lament, "I wonder how they deceived us?"

To me, the important question is, "Are we going to let them deceive us any longer?"

To the true communist, nothing is evil that is expedient. Being without conscience or honor, he feels completely justified in using whatever means are necessary to achieve his goal—force, trickery, lies, broken promises, mayhem and individual and mass murder.

Let us have no illusions about communists. Their leader has told us bluntly—their purpose is not alone to enslave us—they want to bury us.

What we face today is not just a cold war, not just a struggle for the control of land, sea, air, and even outer space, but total competition for the control of men's minds. Unless we meet it and defeat it, we shall almost inevitably one day face the loss of all that we hold dear.

In less than half a century this evil system has gained control over one-third of mankind and it is steadily pursuing its vicious goal of control over all the rest of the world. Since World War II people have been brought under the communist yoke at the rate of more than 6,000 an hour, 144,000 a day, 52,000,000 a year.

Latin America does not believe that suppression is the road to freedom.

Less than fifteen years ago communism was not a powerful force in Latin America. Today it is not only strongly present there as an enemy to be reckoned with—it is openly allied with a government located on an island only about ninety miles south of Key West, Florida.

The only political party now functioning in Cuba is the popular Socialist Party—the Communist Party under another name.

Cuba is being used as a funnel through which communists are infiltrating the other American Republics.

We are dealing with a cunning opponent in Premier Khrushchev. He is a master of deceit. It is he who won in Cuba recently. Premier Khrushchev had taken a tactical "one step backward" by promising to remove Cuban missiles, but this had been followed by the prescribed "two steps forward" when he obtained the claimed promise of the President of the United States that the so-called blockade would be removed . . . and . . . most important, that no one would invade the Cuban islands.

And now, in our latest move, we pay $53 million in goods—plus $2.9 million cash in dishonorable tribute and ransom blackmail to a lying, godless communist dictator.

Why do we, the greatest power in all the world, pay

tribute to an unprincipled tyrant on an island ninety miles away? Why do we bow and scrape to a blustering godless murderer who heads up a freedom-destroying world slave system that is in deep trouble everywhere? Why?

And now close at home—after the ransom and tribute deal—what next for Castro and Cuba? As Americans will we still go gullibly on our complacent way seeking to escape from reality?

The President of the United States (John F. Kennedy) said to the Cuban Freedom Fighters:

"It is the strongest wish of the people of this country, as well as the people of this hemisphere, that Cuba shall one day be free again. . . ."

All true Americans share the President's wish—but it will take much more than wishes to achieve this freedom.

It appears that legally and diplomatically, Cuba has been abandoned to communism—and all of Latin America threatened with this insidious evil.

And now we imprison patriotic exiled Cubans who would fight to deliver their own people from human bondage. This action "has sent a chill of dismay through the hearts of freedom-loving people everywhere."

With our national prestige at or near an all-time low, when will we act like men of courage? Why this continuing policy of softness toward communism? When will we begin to take positions based on what is right and then stand firm? The language and action of firmness will be respected and is the only safe course for our great nation to pursue. When with our national leaders mention, at least, the Monroe Doctrine?

Grassroots thinking in America cries for strong, courageous leadership. The American people are aroused in their hearts. They are far ahead of Washington. They oppose their nation making concessions to Russia. They do not want to be lulled to sleep. The American people are convinced that a firm stand against the communist

masters is the best protection against war. They want to
know the truth without bluffing.

The American public is entitled to the facts. They will
actively follow sound, courageous leadership. Our people
know in their hearts that the opposite of victory is defeat,
whether you call it "coexistence" or "compromise" with a
godless tyranny. We are at war, and we must win the
war. It's time to go on the offensive. Let's stop helping
the enemy of all we hold dear. Let's stop half-measures
such as were used in Cuba. Let us be sure we are right and
then mobilize sufficient strength to win. Let us have no
further blind devotion to the communist-dominated United
Nations. For a change let us try victory.

I have great faith in the American people. When
fully informed, they will make wise decisions. They will
stand up and be counted for what is right. This I know.

I recognize that it is not popular in some circles to be
called an anti-communist, but I consider communism a
political and economic disease. I do not believe an American
citizen can be patriotic and loyal to his own country and
its God-inspired Constitution of freedom without being
anti-communist—anti-socialist.

Now I know that Moscow has ordered that all anti-
communists are to be attacked and discredited in every way
possible. I know the Communist Party of the United States
has issued a similar mandate. This does not disturb me at
all. It should be expected. Meanwhile, we should pursue
a calm and steady course. The path of education to alert
and inform our people "about the methods, purposes and
progress of the conspiracy is the right path. . . . We must
be carefully certain that all we say is the truth, and as re-
strained as circumstances will permit in how we say it.
But to spread the simple childlike truth, about the monstrous
fabrication and falsehoods which make up the very environment of our lives, is a duty to God and country and
family which each of us must assume." (*J. B. S. Bulletin*,

September, 1963.) We are battling against apathy, blind-
ness, opportunism, and propaganda directed brilliantly by
masters of deceit.

We must expose to the light of public inquiry those
forces which would destroy our country and our way of
life. We should pay no attention to the recommendations
of men who call the Constitution an eighteenth century
agrarian document—who apologize for capitalism and free
enterprise. We should refuse to follow their siren song of
concentrating, increasingly, the powers of government in
the Chief Executive, of delegating American sovereign authority to non-American institutions of the United Nations
and pretending that it will bring peace to the world by
turning our armed forces over to a UN world-wide police
force.

"Why do we tear to shreds the historic Monroe Doctrine
which for nearly 140 years has been a cardinal policy of
the US?" (*U.S. News & World Report* 4-15-63.)

This nation needs a revival of patriotism. "Patriotism,"
said Theodore Roosevelt, "means to stand by the country.
It does not mean to stand by the President or any other
public official save exactly to the degree in which he himself stands by the country.

"It is patriotic to support him insofar as he efficiently
serves the country. It is unpatriotic not to oppose him to
the exact extent that by inefficiency or otherwise he fails
in his duty to stand by the country.

"In either event, it is unpatriotic not to tell the truth—
whether about the President or anyone else—save in the
rare cases where this would make known to the enemy information of military value which would otherwise be un-
known to him."

Today as never before, as one courageous patriot has
said, "We want good people, able people, informed people,
determined people, who will live and work and die for what

is right, despite all the misunderstanding and ridicule which such a course may bring upon them; confident and civilized people, who are tolerant of all honest opinions and purposes of others, but eternally intolerant of hypocrisy and cruelty and all the faces of evil. We want men and women, of all races and religious creeds, who believe in the dignity and freedom and responsibility of the individual; who are aware of the follies and crimes of collectivist tyranny; and who are dedicated to man's divinely inspired, ages-long, often frustrated, but ever recurring dream of making this a better world." (*J. B. S. Bulletin*, July, 1963.)

On my desk in Washington, D. C., for eight years as a Cabinet member, I had these words:

"God give us men with a mandate higher than the ballot box."

My heart is filled with gratitude as I witness an ever-increasing group of Americans voluntarily joining together:

1. To combat more effectively the evil forces which now threaten our country, our lives, and our civilization.

2. To prevail upon our fellow citizens to start pulling out of the deepening morass of collectivism, and then climb up the mountain to higher levels of individual freedom and responsibility than man has ever achieved before.

3. To restore with brighter lustre and deeper conviction, the faith-inspired morality, the spiritual sense of values, and the ennobling aspirations, on which our western civilization has been built. (*A Brief Introduction to the J. B. S.*, p. 8.)

I rejoice as I see courageous American patriots stand shoulder to shoulder for "Less government, more responsibility, and a better world."

God grant, that in this blessed land, there will arise "a righteous force, of such mighty strength and such direction that neither the communist conspiracy nor any other agency of Satan can possibly withstand it."

In the world-wide conference of the Mormon Church in April, 1962, President McKay quoted J. Edgar Hoover as follows:

"There is no place here in America for part-time patriots. This nation is face to face with the greatest danger ever to confront it, a sinister and deadly conspiracy which can be conquered only by an alert, informed citizenry. It is indeed appalling that some members of our society continue to deplore and criticize those who stress the communist danger. Public indifference to this threat is tantamount to national suicide. Lethargy leads only to disaster. Knowledge of the enemy, alertness to the danger, everyday patriotism are the brick and mortar with which we can build an impregnable fortress against communism."

Too often in recent years, patriotic symbols have been shunted aside. Our national heroes have been maligned, our history distorted. Has it become a disgrace to pledge allegiance to our flag—or to sign a loyalty oath, or pay tribute to our national anthem? Is it shameful to encourage our children to memorize the stirring words of the men of '76? Has it become opprobrious to state "In God We Trust" when proclaiming love of country?

What we desperately need today is patriotism founded on a real understanding of the American ideal—a dedicated belief in our principles of freedom and a determination to perpetuate America's heritage. . . .

No matter what coloration is put on it, the fact remains that international communism has established a base ninety miles from our shores, from which it is organizing against the United States throughout Latin America.

This contest in which we are engaged is as old as man and as young as hope. This issue is over the God-given eternal principle of freedom—free agency, the right of choice. In this struggle it is not enough to be right—we must put strength and action back of that which is right. In war there is still no substitute for victory.

In the conflict with the world-wide conspiracy we must have patience, courage, and wisdom. We must also have friends. Russia has hostages—we have friends—millions of them in temporary slavery back of the iron curtain, and millions more to be mobilized throughout the free world. In Russia people are unable to challenge the despotic godless dogmas forced on the people. We must take greater risks for freedom. We must dramatize "American might and Soviet myth."

There are some people who hesitate to get into this fight for freedom because it is controversial, or they're not sure if we're going to win.

These people have two blind spots.

First, they fail to realize that life's decisions should be based on principles—not on Gallup polls.

There were men at Valley Forge who weren't sure how the Revolution would end, but they were in a much better position to save their own souls and their country than those timid men whose major concern was deciding which side was going to win, or how to avoid controversy.

After all, the basic purpose of life is to prove ourselves—not to be with the majority when it is wrong.

We must discharge responsibilities not only to our church, home and profession, but also to our country. Otherwise we do not merit the full blessings of a kind Providence.

There are people today all over the world who in their own courageous and sometimes quiet ways are working for freedom. In many cases we will never know until the next life all they sacrificed for liberty. These patriots are receiving heaven's applause for the role they are playing, and in the long run that applause will be louder and longer than any they could receive in this world.

Which leads me to the second blind spot of those who hesitate to get into the fight. And that is their failure to realize that we will win in the long run, and for keeps, and that they pass up great blessings by not getting into the battle now when the odds are against us and the rewards are greatest.

The only questions, before the final victory, are, first, "What stand will each of us take in this struggle?" and second, "How much tragedy can be avoided by doing something now?"

Time is on the side of truth—and truth is eternal.

Those who are fighting against freedom may feel confident now, but they are short-sighted.

This is still God's world. The forces of evil, working through some mortals have made a mess of a good part of it. But it is still God's world. In due time when each of us has had a chance to prove ourselves—including whether or not we are going to stand up for freedom—then God will interject himself, and the final and eternal victory shall be for free agency. And then shall those people on the sidelines, and those who took the wrong but temporarily popular course, lament their decisions.

To the patriots I say this: Take that long eternal look. Stand up for freedom, no matter what the cost.

It can save your soul—and maybe your country.

Yes . . . this is a choice land . . . choice above all others. Blessed by the Almighty, our forebears have made and kept it so. It will continue to be a land of freedom and liberty as long as we are able to advance in the light of sound and enduring principles of right. To sacrifice such principles for momentary expediency—often selfishly motivated—is to endanger our noble heritage and is unworthy of this great American people.

With all my heart I love this great nation. I have lived and traveled abroad just enough to make me appreciate rather fully what we have here. To me this is not just another nation. It is not just one of a family of nations. This is a nation with a great mission to perform for the benefit and blessing of liberty-loving people everywhere. It is my firm conviction that the Constitution of this land was established by men whom the God of heaven raised up unto this very purpose. This is part of my religious faith.

The days ahead are sobering and challenging and will demand the faith, prayers and loyalty of every American.

"The night is far spent, the day is at hand; let us therefore cast off the works of darkness, and let us put on the armour of light." (Romans 13:12.)

May God give us the wisdom to recognize the threat to our freedom and the strength to meet this danger courageously.

Our challenge is to keep America strong and free—strong socially, strong economically, and, above all, strong spiritually, if our way of life is to endure. There is no other way. Only in this course is there safety for our nation.

God grant we may resolutely follow this course in humility and faith, I humbly pray.

(*Hollywood Palladium, Los Angeles, California,* September 28, 1963. *Testimonial Banquet for Mr. Robert Welch.*)

The Internal Threat Today

To you, my friends and former neighbors, I extend my heartfelt appreciation for this cordial welcome. I rejoice to be with you. It would have been a deep disappointment to me if I had missed visiting with you prior to my departure for Europe. My wife and I consider this a choice part of the earth, a place where we have so many friends and so many happy memories of the days when this was our home. God bless all of you!

I am looking forward to this new and challenging assignment of presiding over the European Missions. We will have our headquarters in Frankfurt, Germany, which is one of the oldest cities in Europe. Frankfurt was founded in the first century when Nero was the emperor of Rome. It was the birthplace of Goethe and the home of Martin Luther.

When I visited Germany at the close of World War II, my assignment was to reorganize the church missions and distribute welfare supplies to thousands of destitute people. At that time I found Frankfurt in virtual ruins. Over 10,000 tons of Allied bombs had left only the city's skeleton and that was buried in rubble. Today, however, Frankfurt is completely rebuilt. In fact, it has recaptured its former distinction and is rapidly becoming one of the vital industrial centers of Europe.

In leaving for Europe, I cannot help feeling a very deep sense of anxiety for this great land of America which has just passed through a terrible crisis. To have the President of the United States suddenly torn from his high office by the violent hand of an assassin was an insidious and dastardly act which struck at the very foundation of our Republic.

All of us felt the impact of it. All of us caught the ominous spirit of tragedy and sorrow which accompanied it. Each of us sensed in a very personal way the heartbreak which had come to the Kennedy family.

But after the services and burial were over, we also realized something else. There was the cold, stark reality that the accused assassin's murder of President Kennedy was just one more monstrous treachery in the long list of crimes against humanity which have been inspired down through the years by the godless philosophy of communism.

It was communism that sowed the seeds of treason in the mind of President Kennedy's accused assassin. This is something which must not be forgotten.

In fact, this harsh historical fact should have served as a shock therapy to that segment of our population who like to call themselves "liberals." America is big enough to make room for many different kinds of thinking, but many liberals have claimed to see virtues in socialism and communism which I, for one, have not been able to find. To promote their ideas, American liberals have become a highly organized, hardcore establishment in the United States and they have been excusing their appeasement and coddling of communism on the ground that they were being "tolerant," "broadminded," and "working for peace."

But the assassination of President Kennedy should have jolted them into a realization that they have been pampering, protecting, and promoting the very nest of serpents which produced Lee Harvey Oswald. The diabolical spirit of murder and violence which struck down the President is that same spirit of communist violence which has been allowed to spread its terror into the heart of every continent on the face of the earth. Perhaps those who have been apologists for this conquering Marxist socialist-communist movement might now agree to reconsider the fatal delusion they have been following.

Two additional things happened in connection with this recent tragedy which are worthy of comment.

First was the speed with which the communist leaders

spread the word that the slaying of the President must have been the work of American conservatives. Moscow has conducted a three-year propaganda campaign to make American conservatives look like hysterical fanatics. It has called them "rightists," "extremists," and even "fascists." Within an hour after the assassination, and before Oswald was captured, Moscow was assuring the world that this crime was a product of the "rightist" movement in the United States.

The second thing which happened was the amazing rapidity with which American liberals took up the Moscow line. They too were quick to fix the blame even though there hadn't been the slightest hint as to who had committed the crime. I wonder what would have happened if Oswald had not been captured and identified as an active communist who was in direct contact with party headquarters in New York City? Undoubtedly the liberal element would be blaming this tragedy on conservative Americans to this day.

And even after Oswald was captured and identified as a Moscow-associated communist, there were those who insisted that any who had opposed the President during his term of high office was guilty of that same "spirit of hate" as that which led to the President's death. This line of thinking was expressed by a number of prominent persons through the press, radio, and TV. To me it was incomprehensible.

To equate Oswald's hate and homicidal bitterness with patriotic Americans who happened to oppose some of the policies of the President's administration was the height of distorted and fallacious thinking. The American people can respect their President, pray for their President, even have a strong affection for him, and still have an honest difference of opinion as to the merits of some of his program.

Another recent development has been the call for national unity. I believe there needs to be a unity in our land. But it must not be blind, senseless, irresponsible unity. It should not be guilty just for the sake of unity. It needs to be unity built on sound principles.

We Americans have strayed far from sound principles—morally, constitutionally, and historically. It has been getting us into a quagmire of trouble all over the world, and especially here at home.

Americans at the grassroots level have sensed that their way of life is being threatened. During the last several years there has been a rising tide of resistance to the prevailing political trend. Compromises with communism abroad and flirtations with socialism at home have stirred up opposition in both political parties. And Congress has reflected this opposition. If this has led to disunity, then by all means let us return to a program of sound constitutional principles on which we can unite.

There would be no virtue in calling for unity to support certain legislation if the majority of Americans are opposed to it. And the fact that both Democrats and Republicans in Congress have been resisting certain legislation shows that the executive branch of the government has got out of step with the people.

I believe the American people know what they want. It would appear that the people want their civil rights safeguarded but not a destruction of state's rights.

The farmers want opportunity for security but not agricultural "dictatorship" security.

Parents want better schools for their children but not a Federal subsidy leading to control of the teachings and textbooks as well as the idealogies of the children.

People want sound pay-as-you-go spending with a balanced budget, not reckless spending and tax cuts with an unbalanced budget.

If there is a need for urban renewal, people want it under local direction, not under the red tape of Washington Bureaus armed with confiscatory powers over property.

People want the development of power dams but not

the strangulation of privately owned power companies
which have proved far more efficient and economical than
utilities run by the government.

In other words, there are some legitimate functions and
services which the Federal Government can and should
provide, but those who want the Federal power to exceed
the authority delegated to it by the Constitution will be resisted both by Democrats and Republicans. This is what
has been happening.

And anyone who tires to equate this love of constitutional principles as meaning hatred of our national leaders
is using Goebbels-styled deception. History has already
demonstrated that conservative opposition to national
leaders was not "hate" but an attempt to do them a favor.

Let me give you some examples:

Was it "hate" when General Albert C. Wedemeyer
pleaded with General Marshall and President Truman to
reverse their policy before they lost China?

Was it "hate" when Whittaker Chambers tried to warn
President Roosevelt in 1939 that Alger Hiss had been giving
the Soviet Union more espionage data than any other member of the Washington spy network?

Was it "hate" when J. Edgar Hoover tried to warn
President Truman that Harry Dexter White was a member
of the Soviet spy apparatus and was doing great danger to
the nation as Assistant Secretary of the Treasury?

Was it "hate" when I went to the Secretary of State
under President Eisenhower and pleaded with him not to
support the communist Fidel Castro?

Was it "hate" when the Democratic Senator from Con-
necticut, Thomas Dodd, pleaded for two years with the
President not to support the United Nations' bloodbath
against the free people of Katanga?

This list of acts by well-meaning citizens who wanted
to prevent their Presidents from making serious mistakes
could be extended at length. But they would all illustrate

the same point. History will show that many terrible mistakes occurred because the advice of these well-informed and well-meaning citizens was not heeded.

Therefore, I repeat, this kind of resistance to a national leader is rooted in love and respect, not hate. Regardless of which political party is in power, you do not want to see your President make a serious blunder. You don't want him to lose China. You don't want him to allow the enemy agents to make fools of us. You don't want him to lose Cuba. You don't want him to suffer the humiliation of a "Bay of Pigs disaster," or allow a Soviet Gibraltar to be built ninety miles from our shores.

Every one of those events which have been so disastrous and which have destroyed freedom for hundreds of millions of our allies, could have been prevented. And the voices of those who tried to warn Washington of what was coming cannot be attributed to hate. It has been out of love for our country and respect for our leaders that the voice of warning has been raised.

What causes one to wonder is why these warnings were not carefully considered and acted upon. Why is it that men in high places in Government, regardless of party, have been deceived? I am convinced that a major part of the cause can be justly laid at the door of the socialist-communist conspiracy which is led by masters of deceit who deceive the very elect. J. Edgar Hoover put it well when he said, "I would have no fears if more Americans possessed the zeal, the fervor, the persistence, and the industry to learn about this menace of Red fascism. I do fear for the liberal and progressive who have been hoodwinked and duped into joining the Communists."

Therefore, let those who call for unity and the elimination of hate be sure they are not merely trying to silence the friends of freedom. These are they who respect their leaders and resist them only when it is felt they are headed for a catastrophe. What patriotic American would wish to stand silent if he saw his President verging on a blunder because of bad advice or a mistaken judgment of the facts?

I believe one of the most serious mistakes a President could make would be to weaken the Constitution.

From the time I was a small boy I was taught that the American Constitution is an inspired document. I was also taught that the day will come when the Constitution will be endangered and hang as it were by a single thread. I was taught that we should study the Constitution, preserve its principles, and defend it against any who would destroy it. To the best of my ability I have always tried to do this. I expect to continue my efforts to help protect and safeguard our inspired Constitution.

Recently, however, a critic from Washington claimed that a person who serves in a church capacity should not comment on such matters. He charged that the separation of Church and State requires that church officials restrict their attention to the affairs of the Church.

I, of course, also believe that the institutions of Church and State should be separated, but I do not agree that spiritual leaders cannot comment on basic issues which involve the very foundation of American liberty.

In fact, if this were true, we would have to throw away a substantial part of the Bible. Speaking out against immoral or unjust actions of political leaders has been the burden of prophets and disciples of God from time immemorial. It was for this very reason that many of them were persecuted. Some of them were stoned; some of them were burned; many were imprisoned. Nevertheless, it was their God-given task to speak up.

It is certainly no different today.

To Moses God said: ". . . proclaim liberty throughout all the land unto all the inhabitants thereof." (Lev. 25:10.)

To modern men God has said: the Constitution "should be maintained for the rights and protection of all flesh. . . ." (D & C 101:77.)

Is the Constitution being maintained or is it in jeopardy? Senator J. William Fulbright of Arkansas, says the American Constitution is nothing more than a product of eighteenth century agrarian society. It is now obsolete, he claims. Senator Joseph S. Clark of Pennsylvania says the separation of powers with its checks and balances must be curtailed because they keep the President from making quick and decisive decisions. Gus Hall, head of the Communist Party, USA, agrees with these two Senators and demands that there should be a new Federal Charter eliminating states' rights. America's national sovereignty should be abandoned according to Walt Rostow, Chairman of the State Department Policy Planning Board. He has boldly demanded "an end of nationhood as it has been historically defined." (Quoted in the extension of remarks of Senator Strom Thurmond, *Congressional Record*, June 6, 1963, pp. A3662-3.)

These are some of the same men who see great virtue in a collectivized, socialized society. They want vast powers concentrated in Washington. Samuel Adams of the founding fathers said this was the very thing constitutional government was designed to prevent.

Arthur M. Schlesinger, Jr., is another powerful influence in Washington and a presidential adviser. He not only advocates socialism for the United States but believes that we could eventually form a permanent alliance with communism. He says this would be achieved by having America move to the left while the communists move to the right. We would then meet at the vital center of the socialist-left. The American Constitution, of course, would automatically be discarded.

Arthur Schlesinger and his associates are also opposed to the liberation of the captive nations, even if these nations do it by themselves. These men do not look upon communism as an enemy. They consider communist leaders to be over-zealous allies who will mellow. Therefore, they believe in containing communism, but otherwise supporting it, not thwarting it. They further recommend that wherever communist or socialist regimes are collapsing, we should prop them up . . . feed them, trade with them, grant them loans on long-term credits.

From reading the daily paper you will know that the ideas of these men have already been adopted by Washington as the official policy of the United States.

Now I would say that in a great free country like ours, if these men advocate these suicidal and often treasonable doctrines, shouldn't every patriotic American be free to speak out against them?

At this particular moment in history the United States Constitution is definitely threatened, and every citizen should know about it. The warning of this hour should resound through the corridors of every American institution—schools, churches, the halls of Congress, press, radio, and TV, and so far as I am concerned it will resound—with God's help.

Wherever possible I have tried to speak out. It is for this very reason that certain people in Washington have bitterly criticized me. They don't want people to hear the message. It embarrasses them. The things which are destroying the Constitution are the things they have been voting for. They are afraid of their political careers if these facts are pointed out. They therefore try to silence any who carry the message—anyone who will stand up and be counted.

But these liberal politicians are not the only ones who are trying to silence the warning voice of American patriots. Moscow is equally alarmed.

It was in 1960 when the communist leaders first decided to do something drastic about the rising tide of patriotism in the United States. The loss of Cuba to the Soviet Union had alerted Americans. Citizens were holding study groups, seminars, and freedom schools. The more they studied the more they realized how fast communism was advancing on all fronts. They also learned to their amazement that Washington politicians were doing practically nothing about it. In fact in many cases they were doing things to promote communism. So the protests began to pour into the national capital from every state in the union. All over America there was an awakening.

The Soviet leaders knew this trend could create a crisis for communism, not only in the United States but elsewhere. Therefore, they called together communist delegates from 81 countries and held a meeting in Moscow.

In December, 1960, just three years ago—this communist convention issued an edict that the rising tide of patriotism and anti-communism must be smashed—especially in the United States! All the tricks of hate propaganda and smear tactics were to be unleashed on the heads of American patriots.

Now if the communists had been forced to do this job themselves, it would have been an utter failure. Americans would have simply closed ranks and united. But what mixes up so many people was the fact that the attack on patriotism and the smear of the anti-communist movement did not come in the name of Moscow. It came in the name of influential Americans who espoused the socialist-communist line.

This was a minority bloc of American liberals who formed a propaganda coalition with the communists. Their strategy was ingenious. Almost overnight they drew the line of fire away from the communist conspiracy and focused the heat of attack on the patriots.

How did they do it? They did it by saying that *they* were against the communists but *also* against the anti-communists. They said one was as bad as the other.

Now what kind of logic was this? What if we had taken this approach in the fight against nazism? Informed patriots recognized it as confusion compounded by delusion.

In any event, this deceptive line of propaganda had its impact. These liberal voices would denounce communism and then turn right around and parrot the communist line. They claimed they were anti-communist but spent most of their time fighting those who were really effective anti-communist.

As I asked some of them at the time, "Are you fighting the communists or not? You claim to be fighting the fire, but you spend nearly all of your time fighting the firemen!"

By 1962 these American liberals had almost completely neutralized the resurgence of American patriotism. They had frightened uninformed citizens away from study groups and patriotic rallies. They had made it popular to call patriotism a "controversial" subject which should not be discussed in school assemblies or churches.

From Washington, DC, the Federal Communications Commission issued an edict to radio and television stations that if they allowed the controversial subjects of "Americanism," "Anti-communism," or "States rights," to be discussed on their stations they would be required to give equal time free of charge, to anyone wishing to present an opposite view.

Can you imagine this happening in a free country? I said to my family, "It is fantastic that anything like this could have happened in America."

We should all be opposed to socialistic-communism—for it is our mortal and spiritual enemy. But the reason many liberals don't want the American people to form study groups really to understand and then fight socialistic-communism is that once the American people get the facts, they will begin to realize that much of what these liberals advocate is actually helping the enemy.

The liberals hope you'll believe them when they tell you how anti-communist they are. But they become alarmed if you really inform yourself on the subject of socialistic-communism. For after you inform yourself you might begin to study the liberal voting record. And this study would show you how much the liberals are giving aid and comfort to the enemy and how much the liberals are actually leading America towards socialism itself.

For communism is just another form of socialism, as is fascism. So now you can see the picture. These liberals want you to know how much they are doing for you—with your tax money of course. But they don't want you to realize that the path they are pursuing is socialistic and socialism is the same as communism in its ultimate effect on our liberties. When you point this out, they want to shut you up—they accuse you of maligning them, of casting aspersions, of being political. No matter whether they label their bottle as liberalism, progressivism, or social reform—I know the contents of the bottle is poison to this Republic, and I'm going to call it poison.

We do not need to question the motives of these liberals. They could be most sincere. But sincerity or supposed benevolence or even cleverness is not the question. The question is: "Are we going to save this country from the hands of the enemy and the deceived?"

As J. Edgar Hoover said, "A tragedy of the past generation in the United States is that so many persons, including high-ranking statesmen, public officials, educators, ministers of the Gospel, professional men, have been duped into helping communism. Communist leaders have proclaimed that Communism must be partly built with non-Communist hands, and this, to a large extent, is true." (*Masters of Deceit*, p. 93.)

"We cannot defeat Communism with Socialism, nor with secularism, nor with pacifism, nor with appeasement or accommodation. We can only defeat Communism with true Americanism." (Address by J. Edgar Hoover, Oct. 9, 1962.)

So from the very beginning of this Moscow campaign, to stop the anti-communist movement in this country, it was an important part of the communist strategy to get their liberal American friends to carry out an attack against patriotic organizations. Of course, the communists have learned not to attack all patriotic groups at once. Their strategy is to focus on just one organization and make it so detestable and ugly in the public mind that they can hold it up as a sort of tar baby and then use it to smear all other individuals or groups in the same category.

It was interesting to see just where the communists would begin; which organization would be singled out to get the tar brush treatment. It could have been the American Farm Bureau which the communists have consistently denounced. It could have been the American Legion, Veterans of Foreign Wars, the DAR, or the Sons of the American Revolution. These have been favorite communist targets in the past as had J. Edgar Hoover and the FBI.

As it turned out, it was none of these. Instead, the communists chose to focus their attack on a fairly new organization which very few people had heard about, including myself. They decided to level practically their entire arsenal on the John Birch Society. For the non-political Birch Society had within it, both the policy, the program, and the personnel to help defeat the conspiracy in this country. And the communists knew it, for they had seen its results.

On February 25, 1961, the official communist paper in California, the *People's World*, came out with the opening blast. It said there is a new, secret, fascist society, which is setting up "cells" all over the United States. They said it was the most serious threat to the American way of life.

That was the signal for the bloc of American liberals to take up the torch, and they did. Overnight the patriotic campaign against communism was almost completely forgotten as the liberal vigilantes heroically rode out in full force to save the country from the "terrible Birchers."

Not only the ultra-liberal forces rallied to the battle, but some of the most respected conservative press took up the hue and cry, and many prominent, highly respected Americans also fell for the deceptive line.

The communists had intended to confuse the American people, and they did. The tar brush tactics smeared the image of the new, small, but rapidly growing John Birch Society to the point where many people thought it must be a group of Neo-Nazis or a revival of the Ku Klux Klan.

From the beginning of this attack the John Birch Society pleaded for some kind of official investigation so the truth about them could be given to the public. They believed this was the only way they could counteract the tidal wave of false propaganda which was being heaped upon them. But the investigation was so long in coming that the purposes of the communist-liberal coalition were completely accomplished. It will probably be a long time before the official report on the John Birch Society gets an honest hearing. This investigation was conducted by trained investigators who were working for the California Senate Fact-Finding Committee on un-American Activities. The investigation took two years. Sworn affidavits were obtained from scores of people. The attacks on the society were studied. Interviews were conducted with detractors and supporters of the society. Undetected investigators attended Birch meetings. The Senate Fact-Finding Report was issued in June, 1963.

But even this report was recklessly distorted by some of the liberal press stories. I, therefore, obtained a copy of the report myself so I could see what was in it. The report is 62 pages long, was signed by all members of the committee, and was issued by the President Pro Tem of the California Senate, Senator Hugh M. Burns, a Democrat.

Here are a few quotes:

"... the Society had been publicly charged with being secret, fascist, subversive, un-American, anti-Semitic organization. We have not found any of these accusations to be supported by the evidence.

"We find the John Birch Society to be a Right, anti-Communist, fundamentalist organization. It was conceived, organized and is dominated by Mr. Robert Welch. . . ." (P. 61.)

"We have studied Welch's life, his business career, educational background, and have read almost everything he wrote—all his writings in connection with the Society. . . .
"There is no question as National Review points out, that he has stirred the slumbering spirit of patriotism in thousands of Americans, roused them from lethargy and changed their apathy into a deep desire to first learn the facts about communism and then implement that knowledge with effective and responsible action." (P. 37.)
"We believe that the reason the John Birch Society has attracted so many is that it simply appeared to them to be the most effective, indeed the only organization through which they could join in as a national movement to learn the truth about the Communist menace, and then take some positive concerted action to prevent its spread." (Pp. 61-62.)

This report also goes on to verify what I have already told you, namely, that "The attack against the John Birch Society commenced with an article in the *People's World*, California Communist paper. . . ." (Pp. 25-26.)

Now, in the light of what I have just related, you will understand my feelings when people would ask how I felt about the John Birch Society. Because of the amazingly effective propaganda against them, it has been very unpopular to defend this group. I can remember when it was unpopular to defend my own church. Nevertheless, as soon as I learned what the communists and liberals were doing to the John Birch Society I felt a deep indignation that this should happen to any nonpolitical, patriotic group of American citizens. I felt it was dishonest, immoral, and crass hypocrisy. I still feel that way.

One liberal Congressman attacked the society claiming it was "rotten to the core." Other influential liberals said they objected to the society's "methods." If it was rotten to the core the California Senate fact-finding investigators couldn't discover it.

Some of the finest and best-informed Americans I know have endorsed the society and its program including a number of former FBI agents and officials, counterspies, intelligence and security officers, etc. Many nationally prominent patriotic Americans serve without pay on its council. As to its "methods," the report describes the society as a study group organization designed to "first learn the facts about Communism and then implement that knowledge with effective and responsible action." (P. 37.) What is wrong with such methods as these? It was communists and American liberals who objected to these "methods" because they were effective. They turned out to be traditional American methods that I could find no fault with.

Even in my own Church I found a certain amount of confusion. I heard people say that the LDS Church was opposed to the John Birch Society. This may have come, in part at least, as the result of a statement made by the First Presidency. However, when President McKay discovered that this statement was being misinterpreted and certain people were quoting it to prove the LDS Church was opposing the John Birch Society, he authorized a clarifying statement. This statement appeared in the official Church newspaper for March 16, 1963, and says: "The Church is not opposing the John Birch Society or any other organization of like nature," and "that members of the Church are free to join anti-communist organizations." The statement also says that only one man, President David O. McKay speaks for The Church of Jesus Christ of Latter-day Saints on matters of policy.

Just as a matter of interest you may like to know in a few words what the John Birch Society is and what it stands

for so that you will have a little better idea why some of us
have risen to its defense. Actually what would be better
for you to do would be to read some of their literature for
yourself. Everything the Birch Society publishes is available
to member and non-member alike and their headquarters
at Belmont 78, Massachusetts will be happy to provide this
literature including some other free introductory material.

The society takes its name from one of the greatest
heroes of World War II, Captain John Birch, who was
murdered by the Chinese communists ten days after the war.

The society attempts through an educational and
monthly action program to use every legal and moral means
practicable to preserve our inspired Constitution. These
programs have had a real impact against the conspiracy.
The various programs are purely suggestive and the members are cautioned never to do anything that goes contrary
to their conscience and judgment.

The society is not a political organization—it never
endorses candidates nor contributes to candidates. It en-
courages its members, whether they be Democrats, Republicans, or Independents to study the issues and candidates
in the light of our Constitution and the threats to it and
then govern themselves accordingly.

Among other things the society is for a balanced budget,
for the Monroe Doctrine, and for letting the states solve their
own problems. It is against foreign aid to the communists,
against the Marxist graduated income tax, and against the
federal government competing with tax paying free enterprise. In a sentence, The John Birch Society believes in less
centralized government, more personal responsibility, and
a better world.

I do not belong to the John Birch Society, but I have
always defended this group, just as I do not belong to, but
have defended the American Farm Bureau, the DAR, the
American Legion, the Veterans of Foreign Wars, and any
other patriotic group trying to alert Americans to the so-

cialistic-communist threat. I have also defended J. Edgar Hoover and the FBI.

When my son, Reed, was invited to be a state co-ordinator for the John Birch Society, he asked me if he should accept it. I had read the *Blue Book* and other basic materials of the society. I had met Mr. Welch and other leaders and members. I had read Mr. Welch's famous letter which has since been published in book form entitled *The Politician*. I knew Reed would be enrolling in an unpopular cause. I also knew he would receive a certain amount of vilification if he took this job. Nevertheless, I told him to go ahead, if he thought this was a most effective way to defend the Constitution and fight the socialist-communist menace. I would have given him equal encouragement if he had been considering the FBI or any of our national patriotic organizations dedicated to the fight against the godless conspiracy which threatens all we hold dear.

When he joined, I expressed my opinion that I was convinced that the John Birch Society was the most effective non-church organization in our fight against creeping socialism and godless communism. I also stated that I admire Reed's courage and applauded his decision.

Some people have told me this was not good strategy, but I disagree. I feel it is always good strategy to stand up for the right, even when it is unpopular. Perhaps I should say, *especially* when it is unpopular.

I had to make this same decision all over again just recently. President David O. McKay received an invitation from former Congressman, John Rousselot, asking that I be authorized to give a patriotic speech at a testimonial dinner for Robert Welch. President McKay after careful consideration told me I should take the talk and that I had his permission and blessing. And so the invitation was accepted.

This talk was given at the Hollywood Palladium, September 23rd of this year. (See address "Let Us Live to Make

Men Free.") Nearly 2,000 heard my talk that night, and 4,000 Kiwanians heard a similar message the following day when I spoke at their annual convention.

Both talks dealt with the preservation of the Constitution and the need to resist the communist threat. At the Welch testimonial dinner I commended the John Birch Society and encouraged them to protect the principles of liberty throughout the land.

Of course, as all of you know, this talk brought an immediate outcry from some liberal elements in Washington. These voices said that I, as a church official, had no business speaking at the Robert Welch dinner. They said it was making me "controversial." Patrick Henry and the founding fathers were "controversial," as true patriots have ever been. Perhaps they did not realize that I had filled this assignment with the full approval of President McKay. And perhaps they did not realize that President McKay has not hesitated to speak out for freedom even if some people have considered such patriotism as "controversial." And neither will I hesitate. The fight to save the Constitution is not mere controversy, nor the fight against communism. In fact, it is a war with the devil—Christ versus anti-Christ— and I am willing to fight it.

J. Edgar Hoover has warned that the cold war is a real war and that the threat is increasing. I agree, and unfortunately we're losing the war.

I think it is time for every patriotic American to join with neighbors to study the Constitution and the conspiracy. Subscribe to several good patriotic magazines, buy a few basic books, such as *Masters of Deceit* and *A Study of Communism* by J. Edgar Hoover; *You Can Trust the Communist* by Dr. Fred Schwarz, etc. And then prepare to do some independent thinking. And remember that the organized who have a plan and are dedicated, though they be few, will always defeat the many who are not organized and who lack plans and dedication. The communists know this and have proved it. Isn't it about time that most Americans realized it too?

One of our most serious problems is the inferiority complex which people feel when they are not informed and organized. They dare not make a decision on these vital issues. They let other people think for them. They stumble around in the middle of the road trying to avoid being "controversial" and get hit by traffic going both ways.

In this mighty struggle each of you has a part. Every person on the earth today chose the right side during the war in heaven. Be on the right side now. Stand up and be counted. If you get discouraged, remember the words of Edward Everett Hale when he said:

> "I am only one, but I am one
> I can't do everything, but I can do something.
> What I can do, that I ought to do.
> And what I ought to do
> By the grace of God, I shall do!"

And this is my prayer for you this day. May God bless all of you, each and every one.

(*Boise High School Auditorium, Boise, Idaho*, December 19, 1963.)

We Must Become Alerted and Informed

This is a signal honor, a very great pleasure and a challenging responsibility. My gratitude for this opportunity is increased by the realization that it may be several months —possibly years—before I come to this lovely Cache Valley again. I love this valley. Here I was born in a choice home and reared to manhood. Here in this very community I met, courted, and won my choice companion who has been a constant inspiration and support to me. Yes, this is home country.

I am grateful for the call which has come to me again to preside over the European Mission, even though I leave my beloved country this time with greater anxiety for its future than ever before.

Because of the nature of the message I bring to you tonight I have committed most of it to writing. I shall speak to you frankly and honestly. Some of you may not agree with everything I say. Thank God in this blessed land we can still speak our convictions without fear. I have been in nations where this blessed privilege is no longer enjoyed.

These are my personal convictions borne out of an active life which has taken me into forty-five nations and brought me close to the insidious forces which would destroy our way of life.

J. Edgar Hoover in his sobering address, *Communist Target—Youth*, warns us that, "The menace of communism is not a simple forthright threat. Instead, it is a conspiracy which can be controlled only through full understanding of the true nature of the conspiracy and the ability to separate truth from propaganda. Only our apathy and laxity in the face of the threat which communist infiltration efforts represent can cause such a failure. It is the duty of all

Americans to fully understand the true import of this threat to our heritage, to expose it, and to combat it with every weapon at our command." (Pp. 10-11.)

President David O. McKay has warned us time and time again that there is present in our own United States "influences the avowed object of which is to sow discord and contention among men with a view of undermining, weakening, if not entirely destroying, our constitutional form of government. . . . It is the enemy from within," warns this great leader, "that is most menacing, especially when it threatens to disintegrate our established forms of government."

For a quarter of a century I have seen, at close range, the insidious forward march of creeping socialism and its ruthless companion godless communism. It is a shocking record of bluff, bluster, deception, intrigue, bondage, and mass murder. Never in recorded history has any movement spread itself so far and so fast as has socialistic-communism in the past few years. The facts are not pleasant to review. Communist leaders are jubilant with their success. They are driving freedom back on almost every front.

Do you realize that the first communist cell in our government, so far as we know, was organized in the United States Department of Agriculture in the 1930's? John Abt was there. Lee Pressman was there. Harry Dexter White was there. Yes, and Alger Hiss was there. In less than half a century this evil system has gained control over one-third of mankind, and it is steadily pursuing its vicious goal of control over all the rest of the world.

But the Communist Party and its fellow travelers and sympathizers are "manifestly frightened by the possibility of the people of the U. S. becoming awakened. Communist success has always been achieved in an atmosphere of secrecy, deceit and confusion." (*The Communist Attack on the John Birch Society*, p. 12. Skousen.) Therefore, courageous organizations and individuals that are successful in awakening the American people are marked for annihilation.

The smear seems to be the most widely used and effective tool of the conspiracy to discredit and weaken any effective anti-communist effort. The smear of any individual or organization by the communists, their dupes, and fellow travelers is certain evidence of effectiveness. If any of you are affiliated with patriotic organizations reportedly opposed to the communist conspiracy, which are not extensively smeared, you can rest assured your opposition is largely ineffective. You had best look for a more fruitful affiliation.

It seems almost unbelievable that 52 million liberty-loving people could be brought under communist bondage each and every year since World War II. Why this shocking record? How could this happen? How can men, many of them in high places, who seem to be so strong for Christian principles and basic American concepts be so effectively used to serve the communist conspiracy? How can our own people be lulled away into a false security crying, "All is well"?

I believe the answer is found in the fact that these godless communist conspirators and their gullible fellow travelers are masters of deceit—who deceive the very elect.

I quote the great American, J. Edgar Hoover: "I confess to a real apprehension so long as communists are able to secure ministers of the gospel to promote their evil work and espouse a cause that is alien to the religion of Christ and Judaism. I do fear so long as school boards and parents tolerate conditions whereby communists and fellow travelers under the guise of academic freedom can teach our youth a way of life that eventually will destroy the sanctity of the home, that undermines faith in God, that causes them to scorn respect for constituted authority and sabotage our revered Constitution." (*Menace of Communism*, p. 11.)

Our complacency as a nation is shocking—yes, almost unbelievable!

We are a prosperous nation. Our people have high-paying jobs. Our incomes are high. Our standard of living is at an unprecedented level. We do not like to be disturbed as we enjoy our comfortable complacency. We live in the soft present and feel the future is secure. We do not worry about history. We seem oblivious to the causes of the rise and fall of nations. We are blind to the hard fact that nations usually sow the seeds of their own destruction while enjoying unprecedented prosperity.

I say to you with all the fervor of my soul: We are sowing the seeds of our own destruction in America and much of the free world today. It is my sober warning to you today that if the trends of the past thirty years—and especially the past three years—continue, we will lose that which is as priceless as life itself—our freedom—our liberty —our right to act as free men. It can happen here. It is happening here.

Our greatest need in America today is to be alerted and informed. When we have become alerted and informed, we will soberly sense the need for a reversal of the present trends. We will realize that the laws of economics are immutable. We will be convinced that we must return to a spirit of humility, faith in God and the basic concepts upon which this great Christian nation has been established under the direction of Divine Providence.

We must return to a realization of the source of our strength. Then and only then will we be able to see clearly American might and Soviet myth. Then will we realize the truth of what President George Albert Smith said that, "The Constitution of the United States of America is just as much from my Heavenly Father as the Ten Commandments." (*Conf. Report* April 1948, p. 182.)

The sad and shocking story of what has happened in America in recent years must be told. Our people must have the facts. There is safety in an informed public. There is real danger in a complacent, uninformed citizenry. This is our real danger today. Yes, the truth must be told even at the risk of destroying, in large measure, the influence of men who are widely respected and loved by the American people. The stakes are high. Freedom and survival is the issue.

Today we are at war. It is not enough to be against communism. We must shed our complacency and aggressively meet this challenge. . . . There can be no compromise with the communists. They are at war with us—with the entire cause of freedom, and the sooner every American faces this hard fact, the stronger our position will be. It is a real war. The lines are tightly drawn. The war is more insidious, more devious, more devastating, and more satanical than any war in our history. Moral principles, once universally recognized are ignored. International law once respected is thrown to the wind.

The socialist-communist philosophy is devastatingly evil—destructive of all that is good, uplifting and beautiful. It strikes at the very foundation of all we hold dear. The communist "has convinced himself that nothing is evil which answers the call of expediency." This is a most damnable doctrine. People who truly accept such a philosophy have neither conscience nor honor. Force, trickery, lies, broken promises to them are wholly justified.

We believe in religion as a mode of life resulting from our faith in God. Communism contends that all religion must be overthrown because it inhibits the spirit of world revolution. Earl Browder, a long-time leader of the Communist Party in the USA said, ". . . we Communists do not distinguish between good and bad religions, because we think they are all bad."

This atheistic, degrading, but militant philosophy is backed up with the strength and resources of a big country of 210 million people and a militaristic economy. In addition, communism has built an empire of 700 million more slaves. Besides this, it has agents in all free world countries whose ultimate aim is to overthrow the existing social order and bring these countries under the red flag. And yet in the face of all this, we gullibly sign treaties and accept promises of these godless murderers. When will we as a people awake to the awful threat which faces us? It must be soon or it will be too late. Already it is the eleventh hour.

The socialist-communist pattern and objective is being followed and achieved. The record is clear, especially the fantastic and terrifying communist advance and conquest of the past ten years. What will the world look like in another decade?

Lenin died in 1924. But before he died, he had laid down for his followers the strategy for this conquest. It was, we should readily admit, brilliant, farseeing, realistic, and majestically simple. It has been paraphrased and summarized as follows: "First, we will take Eastern Europe. Next, the masses of Asia. Then we shall encircle that last bastion of capitalism, the United States of America. We shall not have to attack; it will fall like overripe fruit into our hands."

As recent as ten years ago most Americans, even some who were fairly well informed, did not know and would not believe that there was any such thing as a socialist-communist conspiracy. Today some of these same people will solemnly argue as to whether we have five years or maybe ten years before we too are living as slaves in a communist police state. They now realize *it can happen here.*

How did it all come about? Time will not permit details. However, the record of planned intrigue, deception and murder is available for all to see and read. The record is clear. Just a few highlights will suffice.

The first real great break for the communist conspiracy came in 1933. The United States formally recognized Stalin's godless, murderous regime. We extended diplomatic relations to atheistic Russia. I believed it to be a mistake then, and I am more convinced of it than ever today. Our recognition of Russia in 1933 tremendously increased their standing, prestige, and credit, at home and with other nations. It saved them from financial collapse; and it enabled them greatly to increase their nests of spies and propaganda agents in this country and elsewhere in the world.

And we've been bailing them out of their difficulties and bolstering their slave economy ever since. They have repudiated the hundreds of millions owed to the U.S. before World War II and have deceptively withheld, even an expression of gratitude for more than eleven billion dollars worth of food, supplies, war materials, etc., under lend-lease. And we're still at it. Now it's wheat. Soft on communism did someone say?· No free nation has ever been more gullibly soft on this godless conspiracy than our own beloved but foolhardy nation.

Their second great break came with the beginning of World War II, which was largely brought on through the world-wide diplomatic conniving of Stalin's agents, making Russia a wartime ally of the Western nations, thereby providing the resulting opportunities for communism through the chaos of war.

During the war and post-war period communist agents kept the eyes and anger of the world focused on the crimes of Hitler. At the same time, Stalin, with his aim on Lenin's objectives carried out conquest and crime, continuously and successfully, that far outdid even Hitler's dreams. The record now began to be plain to see.

August, 1939, Poland was betrayed and the eastern portion seized. In 1940 communism took over part of liberty-loving and America-loving Finland. Communism also swallowed up Estonia, Latvia, and Lithuania. Later at the Teheran Conference in 1943 with Alger Hiss, the communist, as the principal adviser to President Franklin

Roosevelt, it was made clear Stalin would be allowed to keep all and everything he had stolen.

Then a new series of conquests started. 1946: Albania, Hungary, Yugoslavia, Romania, and Bulgaria. 1947: the mock elections in Poland formally completed the two years of incredibly cruel subjection of this traditional liberty-loving nation. Then in February, 1948, Czechoslovakia, created with the help of our own President Woodrow Wilson, fell. In October, 1950 Stalin's agents formalized their puppet state of East Germany. This finished the job as planned by Lenin twenty-six years earlier. The ruthless communist conspiracy now had Eastern Europe entire, and the first step of their infamous three-step program was complete.

Step two was Asia. The record clearly indicates that while achieving step one in Eastern Europe, the communist masters were planning and working on step two to enslave Asia. The infiltration of China was already well advanced. Mao and the Chinese communists were already crushing their opposition. A prominent actor in this heart-rending drama was the great patriot, Chiang Kai-shek. General George Marshall also played a major but tragic role. His contribution was to help the communists. By 1950 the whole mainland of China was enslaved.

1951 saw Moscow's invaders seize Tibet. Then in the summer of 1953 the shameful action in Korea, so incredible in the light of past American history. Then in 1954 the better half of Indochina!

Then the blackout was temporarily slowed by Stalin's passing, but the conspiracy continued forward towards ultimate total victory. We also witnessed the effective use of the so-called neutralists of which Sukarno, like Cuba's Castro, is an example, and who, like Castro, a few years ago was referred to by American leaders as the George Washington of Indochina.

It is frightening to note the extent to which the goals

announced by the communist masters have been achieved and with American aid. Again I repeat their bold strategy:

"First, we will take Eastern Europe. Next, the masses of Asia. Then we will encircle that last bastion of capitalism, the United States of America. We shall not have to attack; it will fall like overripe fruit into our hands."

Coming to the Western Hemisphere what do we find? The communist, godless, insidious conspiracy is moving forward at a shocking pace. There are very few remaining really anti-communist governments in Latin America. The growing communist infiltration and influence right inside our own continental borders has become alarming. It is particularly alarming to those who know the extent of the problem. And to the great majority of the American people—uninformed as they are—it is not believed. And therein lies the real danger.

Who would have believed in 1953, for instance, that in just ten years Cuba would be a slave state in the communist empire—a military and political base for the continuing infiltration, subversion, and attack of all of Latin America? Or that certain officials in our own government would have helped so effectively to betray Cuba into communist hands by following almost exactly the same pattern as that which was used in the earlier betrayal of China? And who would have believed ten years ago that the American people, only ninety miles away, would have been so conditioned by further years of pro-communist brainwashing that they would stand passively by accepting these developments without demanding appropriate drastic action?

Who would have believed that State Department officials and Presidents of the United States would refuse to confirm the historic and inspired Monroe Doctrine—the center of our foreign policy for 140 years? Who would have believed our own State Department would refer to a godless, blustering dictator as the "great liberator of the

Cuban people"? Who would have believed that the American press would fall for the deceptive line of the communist conspiracy—even calling Castro the "George Washington of Cuba"?

There is no greater evidence today of American complacency than this. Yes, we have been lulled away into a false security. We are busy making money, enjoying our abundance but oblivious to the gradual loss of our freedom which has made all of these blessings possible. As a nation we are affluent but foolish.

This nation needs a revival of patriotism, a return to basic concepts, an awakening to the most deadly peril ever to threaten our people. I say to you with all my heart that the danger is real and can be deadly. We must become *alerted and informed.*

With our national prestige at or near an all-time low, when will we act like men of courage? Why this continuing policy of softness toward communism? When will we begin to take positions based on what is right and then stand firm? The language and action of firmness will be respected and is the only safe course for our great nation to pursue. When will our national leaders mention at least, the Monroe Doctrine?

Grassroots thinking in America cries for strong, courageous leadership. Some American people are at long last becoming aroused in their hearts. They are far ahead of most Washington politicians. They oppose their leaders making concessions to Russia. They do not want to be lulled to sleep. The American people are convinced that a firm stand against the communist masters is the best protection against war. They want to know the truth without bluffing.

The American people are entitled to the facts. They will actively follow sound, courageous leadership. Our people know in their hearts that the opposite of victory is defeat, whether you call it "coexistence" or "compromise" with a godless tyranny.

We are at war, and we must win the war. It's time to go on the offensive. Let's stop helping the enemy. Let's stop half-measures such as were used in Cuba. Let's be sure we're right and then mobilize sufficient strength to win. For a change let's try victory!

I have great faith in the American people. When fully informed they will make wise decisions. They will stand up and be counted for what is right. This I know. I agree with sentiments expressed by one of our fine patriots, Tom Anderson: "As Americans we must stand up and be counted —else we'll be counted out. . . . The middle of the road between the extremes of good and evil is evil. When freedom is at stake, our silence is not golden, it's yellow. . . . Why change the American system which produced the greatest freedom for the greatest number of people in human history, along with the world's highest standard of living, for socialism. . . . Under any name socialism has been a miserable failure for 1,000 years. . . . A government big enough to give you everything you want is big enough to take everything you've got."

Ten years ago the American people did not dream that the communist advance was getting so near home as to threaten the very take-over of Central and South America. Yet today you can count on the fingers of one hand all the countries, in the whole continent and subcontinent together, where the communists do not exercise dominant influences in the governments. Does this concern us as United States citizens? Again I say it can happen here. And apparently some American people are ready to accept what ten years ago they would not have considered even possible. Yes, it can—it is happening here.

Who would have believed ten years ago that the Supreme Court of the United States would have wilfully and disastrously punched large ragged holes in our God-inspired

Constitution? Who would have believed the Court would have handed down so many decisions favorable to the communists and so weakening and destructive of our protection against them, that the communists themselves would openly declare certain of these decisions to be the greatest victory ever won by the communists in America.

Who would have believed ten years ago that a great patriot and beloved spiritual leader would warn us that a recent decision of our Supreme Court is leading this nation down the road to atheism?

Who would have believed ten years ago that the conference of Chief Justices of our state supreme courts would have been so disturbed by this usurpation of power by the Supreme Court as to say things about the Warren-led Supreme Court as harsh as anything that has been said by even the so-called "extreme rightists," who in reality are real patriots in the spirit of Patrick Henry and the founding fathers?

Who would have believed that Washington politicians would be openly and brazenly sending American wealth in quantities of many billions to aid avowed communists? Or that the United States would be discouraging Soviet satellites from thinking of revolt and advising them to accept their status quo and make the best of their subservient relationship to Moscow without trying to change it.

Who would have believed ten years ago that the President of the U.S. would be holding futile summit conferences with the murderous lords of the Kremlin; fraternizing with, and honoring as a guest of this nation, our arch enemy and master murderer of all time, Nikita Khrushchev.

And who would have imagined that within ten years another President of the United States would support and get passed legislation making it the official policy of the United States to turn over our own armed forces into the hands of the United Nations, already visibly controlled by the communists and their dependencies? And yet that legislation has been on our statute books since September 1961. The only question now is how fast the administration dares to implement it.

In view of all these and other facts one might well ask: America, what of the future?

And now a President of the United States has been assassinated by a communist within the borders of the United States. Will a nation in deep mourning rededicate itself to the fight against the godless communist conspiracy? With cool heads and unwavering confidence and courage let us each do our part to become alerted and informed—to fight and defeat this godless conspiracy.

What will the next ten years bring? Careful students of this problem, caused by the communist conspiracy, conclude that at the present rate of communist progress, the struggle will, in ten years, be over. Communist control, these authorities believe, will be visibly complete everywhere in the world except in North America and will actually be complete here in fact, if not in obvious form. Certainly, they say by 1973, unless Americans become alerted, informed, and take effective anti-communist action, the full scourge of brutal communistic tyranny will be in effect all over the country. This, they say, will include military occupation, concentration camps, tortures, terror and all that is required to enable about three percent of the population to rule the other ninety-seven percent as slaves. For achieving that "power and glory" throughout the world is, of course, the real purpose of communism. All else is mere pretense and deception on their part.

As, and if, we move towards that condition there will be a gradual further loss of our freedom, an increase of the inducements for the acceptance of communism, and a corresponding increase of the pressures to destroy or remove all opponents and all opposition to the communist advance.

There would be a further huge expansion of government and of its control over our economy, education, medical services, and every detail of our family and individual lives.

During such a period, it is reasonable to expect—unless sufficient brakes are put on the present stampede to the left, we will get exactly what the communist-socialist coalition is planning—the nationalization of insurance, transportation, communications, utilities, banks, farms, housing, hospitals, and schools. To take over our schools the educational system will first have been federalized and then prostituted entirely to serving the propaganda needs of the state planners with absolutely no regard for truth or scholarship or tradition.

Fantastic, you say?

Impossible? Not so long ago I personally heard the people of Czechoslovakia, Cuba, Poland, express similar assurances, that the communist conspiracy would not take them over. But it did happen. Bondage did come. Freedom was lost.

No, I do not predict—nor do the experts—that all these tragic things must come to pass within ten years. I do say, however, that such is clearly indicated unless something is done to slow up, stop or reverse present communist progress in this hemisphere and particularly in the United States.

I expect to continue to pray, speak, and act with all my energy, and I hope you do also, to prevent the tragedy in America which has come to many other once free lands. At present, unless we join with those small but determined and knowledgeable patriots, dedicated to preserve our freedom, a cold calculation would show that we will not be able to change the course of the present ominous and shocking trends in our beloved country.

As I leave the shores of this choice land, it is my hope and prayer that the American people can be awakened sufficiently from their sleep of complacency—that they will become alerted and informed. It is also my hope and prayer that more will join forces with those who are opposing the conspiracy in an effective organization. Words will not stop the communists. We must be neither fatalists nor pessimists. We must be realists, of high character and deep spirituality.

It has been carefully estimated that since August, 1945, the communists have averaged taking over about seven thousand newly enslaved subjects every hour. And please remember that these people, whether in Indonesia or Iraq or Korea, have the same love for their families, think of concentration camps with the same despairing horror, and feel the same pain under torture, as do you and I.

So let me repeat that. Seven thousand more human beings just like you and me have been brought under the incredibly brutal rule of a communist police state, *every hour*, twenty-four hours of every day, 365 days of every year, for the past eighteen years. And not only is that process not being interrupted in any way. Today the rate of conquest and enslavement is actually increasing. The number of slave labor camps has increased under Khrushchev compared to Stalin. Yet some gullible, fuzzy heads are trying to tell us that the communists are changing—becoming more co-operative. They might change their strategy, but their objective is still to "bury us." Their deadly conspiracy remains the same.

"Now please note that the Communists have never made any of this immense progress by the direct use of force. They have beguiled Chinese into fighting Chinese, Koreans into fighting Koreans, Vietnamese into fighting the French and each other, the Israelis, British and French into fighting Egyptians, and the Algerians into fighting the French. They have even maneuvered Americans into fighting Chinese Communists in Korea, with the Americans' hands tied behind their backs. But not one Russian regiment has ever taken part in any of this imperialistic advance, except in the suppression of rebellion in already conquered territory, as in Hungary. The Communists have put over these tremendous gains by bluff and bluster, lies and deception, murder, and—above all—by treason within our governments and by diplomatic pressures based on all of these other means. And that lamp of experience certainly should guide us as to what they are up to today." (*Blue Book*, J. B. S., p. 27.)

There are three possible methods by which the communists might take us over. One would be through a sufficient amount of infiltration and propaganda, to disguise communism as just another political party.

The second method would be by fomenting internal civil war in this country, and aiding the communists' side in that war with all necessary military might.

The third method would be by a slow insidious infiltration resulting in a take over without the American people realizing it.

The Soviets would not attempt military conquest of so powerful and so extensive a country as the United States without availing themselves of a sufficiently strong fifth column in our midst, a fifth column which would provide the sabotage, the false leadership, and the sudden seizures of power and of means of communication, needed to convert the struggle, from the very beginning, into a civil war rather than clear-cut war with an external enemy.

We can foresee a possibility of the Kremlin taking this gamble in time. In fact, it is clear that the communists long ago made plans to have this method available, in whole or in part, to whatever extent it might be useful. The trouble in our southern states has been fomented almost entirely by the communists for this purpose. It has been their plan, gradually carried out over a long period with meticulous cunning, to stir up such bitterness between the whites and blacks in the South that small flames of civil disorder would inevitably result. They could then fan and coalesce these little flames into one great conflagration of civil war, in time, if the need arose.

The whole slogan of "civil rights" as used to make trouble in the South today, is an exact parallel to the slogan of "Agrarian reform" which they used in China. The pending "civil rights" legislation is, I am convinced, about 10% civil rights and about 90% a further extension of socialistic Federal Controls. It is part of the pattern for the Communist take over of America. "The whole civil rights" program and slogan in America today is just as phony as were the "Agrarian reform" program and slogan of the communists in China 20 years ago.

But the third method is far more in accordance with Lenin's long-range strategy. It is one which they are clearly relying on most heavily. And this is taking us over by a process so gradual and insidious that Soviet rule is slipped over so far on the American people, before they ever realize it is happening, that they can no longer resist the communist conspiracy as free citizens, but can resist the communist tyranny only by themselves becoming conspirators against established government. The process in that direction is going on right now, gradually but surely and with ever-increasing spread and speed.

A part of that plan, of course, is to induce the gradual surrender of American sovereignty, piece by piece and step by step, to various international organizations.

Communism is not a political party, nor a military organization, nor an idealogical crusade, nor a rebirth of Russian imperialist ambition, though it comprises and uses all these. Communism, in its unmistakable reality, is wholly a conspiracy, a gigantic conspiracy to enslave mankind; an increasingly successful conspiracy, controlled by determined, cunning and utterly ruthless gangsters, willing to use any means to achieve its end.

Today as never before, America has need for men and women who possess the moral strength and courage of our forefathers—modern-day patriots, with pride in our country and faith in freedom.

"What we *desperately* need today is patriotism founded on a real understanding of the American ideal—a dedicated belief in our principles of freedom and a determination to perpetuate America's heritage. . . . There must be in America a rebirth of the spirit of Valley Forge. . . ." (J. Edgar Hoover.)

We are losing, rapidly losing, a cold war in which our freedom, our country, and our very existence are at stake. And while we do not seem to know we are losing this war, you can be sure the communists do. They realize it fully and they are jubilant with their success. There is just one thing—only one thing in the whole world—which the communists fear today. It is that, despite their tremendous influence in our government and over all of our means of mass communication—they fear that the American people will wake up too soon to what has really been happening and what is now happening right under their very noses.

The only thing which can possibly stop the communists is for the American people to learn the truth in time—to become alerted and informed.

There are some seven hundred million non-Russians, non-communists now living daily lives of virtual slavery behind the Iron Curtain, some forty million of them in the actual slave labor camps of Russia and Red China. These good people only a dozen years ago, more or less, enjoyed practically the same personal freedom as do you and I today. These people now say to each other, but above all to themselves: "If I had only known! If I had only believed! If I had only been alert and informed!"

This is a world-wide battle, the first of its kind in history, between light and darkness; between freedom and slavery; between the spirit of Christianity and the spirit of anti-Christ for the souls and bodies of men. Let's win that battle by alertness, by determination, by courage, by an energizing realization of the danger, if we can; but let's win it even with our lives, if the time comes when we must.

God grant that the United States of America may become alerted and informed and provide the courageous leadership so desperately needed in the world today. Then the enslaved people everywhere would start throwing off their shackles. And God grant that the restoration of freedom and honor and sanity to the conduct of human affairs will begin before the godless communist conspiracy destroys our civilization.

What a glorious day it would be to see America, a land choice above all other lands, exert her power and leadership. America, the greatest nation under heaven, is the hope of the free world, and the hope for the slaves of despotism. This nation is the only effective deterrent to total communist slavery. We can prevent it. We can restore and preserve freedom.

Imagine the joy of mankind living in a free world once again, as brothers, as the God of heaven would have us do. That it may again be realized in our day, is my humble prayer.

(*Logan Tabernacle, Logan, Utah,* December 13, 1963.)

A Race against Time

This morning I will dispense with the usual amusing story so often told at the beginning of a speech. I do this because time is so rapidly running out that I feel I must have your ears during every moment of the time allotted to me. I do not mean that the hour is late today. I do mean that the hour is very late indeed, on the time table of national survival. As Ernst Tillich stated in his testimony as an expert witness before the House Committee on Un-American Activities several years ago: "On the clock of survival the time is now five minutes before midnight. We have but this brief interval to choose between survival or extinction."

The events which have taken place since Mr. Tillich testified have fully supported this grave warning. We have been plunging headlong down the primrose path toward the inevitable destruction of our great country. It is quite true that while the socialist-communist conspiracy, of itself, does not have, as yet, the power necessary to do the job, it is nevertheless receiving vital aid and comfort from the Fabian socialists, fellow travelers, dupes and liberals, to such a degree that the communists are jubilant at the course of events.

In less than half a century this evil system has gained control over one-third of mankind, and it is steadily pursuing its vicious goal of control over all the rest of the world. Truly, the Fabian socialists in this country are rolling out the red carpet, which will, without a doubt, unless we arouse ourselves, eventually result in a complete communist take-over of America. This is their hope, their plan, and their bold prediction.

This is not to say that all those lending their support to the Fabian socialist camp are consciously helping the

communists. Undoubtedly there are many well-meaning people who have been misled or confused. However, it makes little difference who pulls the trigger of a gun aimed at your heart. The end result is the same.

There are real dangers ahead. Why do I have anxiety and fear for the future?

I fear for the future when I realize that for some thirty years our once-free institutions, political, economic, educational and social, have been drifting into the hands of those who favor the welfare state, and who would "centralize all power in the hands of the political apparatus in Washington. This enhancement of political power at the expense of individual rights, so often disguised as 'democracy' or 'freedom' or 'civil rights,' is 'socialism,' no matter what name tag it bears.

"Here we should recall the warning of the late Dean Inge: 'History seems to show that the powers of evil have won their greatest triumphs by capturing the organizations which were formed to defeat them, and that when the devil has thus changed the contents of the bottles, he never alters the labels. The fort may have been captured by the enemy, but it still flies the flag of its defenders.'" (Admiral Ben Moreell, November 22, 1963.)

I fear for the future when the central government now owns more than one-third of the total land area within the boundaries of the fifty states.

I fear for the future when the central government owns and operates more than 3,000 businesses and commercial activities in competition with its own private taxpaying citizens.

I fear for the future when I realize that the functions of the Federal Government are carried on by some 2,000 major operating units.

I fear for the future when the Federal Government directly lends $1 for every $5 lent by private banks and that much of the federal funds lent are at rates below the cost of the money to the government.

I fear for the future when in 1913-15 a couple making $10,000, paid in federal taxes $60, but in 1956 a couple earning $10,000 paid $1,590 in federal income tax.

I fear for the future when I realize that twenty-five years ago the Federal Government received one-fourth of all taxes collected in the United States. Today the Federal Government collects not one-quarter but 68 percent of all our taxes.

I fear for the future when foreign governments have used and are using American tax money to pay for socialism.

I fear for the future because twenty-five years ago all taxes, federal, state and local, took 14 percent of our national income. Today taxes take 35 percent.

I fear for the future when I see our federal debt soar well above 300 billion dollars—over $7,000 per family of four—sixteen times the combined debt of the fifty states and at the same time see no evidence that this dangerous trend will be curtailed.

I fear for the future when I see an affluent but complacent citizenry paying little or no attention to these and many other socialistic trends in America.

Dr. V. Orval Watts, noted political economist, has described this socialist system which I fear—and I have but suggested a very few evidences. Here are his words:

"Socialism . . . is the theory and practice of coercive collectivism. It is the evil fruit of greed for other men's possessions and greed for control over other men's labor.

"This greed for goods and power is as old as man and as widespread as the human race. It goes by many names, disguised in many forms, as men think up many excuses for robbing and ruling their fellows.

"Socialist theory is a modern excuse, an elaborate rationalization for this greed and for the organized looting and despotism it seeks to achieve. But its materialism, its collectivist point of view, its reliance on violence and coercion, even most of its economics, are as old and as common as sin.

"It holds out to men the hope that they may reap where they have not sown. It teaches that man is the creature of his environment, and that he may be happy and good if he gets enough wealth, regardless of how or where. All that is needed, says the socialist tempter, is to bow down and worship the socialist state, turning over to it authority and power to take wealth where it finds it and to direct labor as it wills. Just a little class hatred, a little lying propaganda, a little violence on the picket lines, a little supression of adverse critics, and a few generations of compulsory education in socialistic thought, then surely we shall see the bright new day of equality, peace, brotherhood, and freedom! So says the Socialist."

In 1878, the great Southern statesman, Benjamin Hill of Georgia, warned us of these dangers on the floor of the United States Senate, in these prophetic words:

"I dread nothing so much as the exercise of ungranted and doubtful powers by this Government. It is, in my opinion, the danger of dangers to the future of this country. Let us be sure that we keep it always within its limits.

"If this great, ambitious, ever-growing corporation becomes aggressive, who shall check it? If it becomes wayward, who shall control it? If it becomes unjust, who shall trust it? As sentinels of the country's watchtower, I beseech you to watch and guard with sleepless dread that corporation which can make all property and rights, all states and people, and all liberty and hope, its playthings in an hour, and its victims forever."

Admiral Ben Moreell, who has spoken here, has wisely declared:

"We do not place our trust in government mechanisms, formulas, affirmations or men. Our faith is in God and in the capacity of free men and women to govern themselves. There is a proper function for government in a free society. But that function does not include the power to order citizens how to live their lives. Our government was not designed to administer the affairs of men; it was devised to administer justice among men, who would administer their own affairs."

That great and wise American, Thomas Jefferson, warned us of the danger of conferring unwarranted power upon our government administrators in these sobering words:

"It would be a dangerous delusion, were a confidence in the men of our choice, to silence our fears for the safety of our rights. Confidence is everywhere the parent of despotism. Free government is founded in jealousy, and not in confidence. It is jealousy and not confidence which prescribes limited constitutions, to bind down those whom we are obliged to trust with power; our Constitution has accordingly fixed the limits to which, and no further, our confidence may go. . . . In questions of power, then, let not more be heard of confidence in man, but bind him down from mischief by the chains of the Constitution."

We are now—this very day—at war with the socialist-communist conspiracy. This is a point that a lot of people do not seem to realize. They think that just because we are not shooting at each other with bullets that it isn't a real war. But, we are really at war and we must win this war if we expect to survive as a free people. The following quotations by J. Edgar Hoover point this out clearly:

"We are at war with the communists and the sooner every redblooded American realizes this the safer we will be. . . . We are living in an age of uncertainty—an age of awesome national peril—an age when the struggle between freedom and totalitarian enslavement is drawing toward a climax." (J. Edgar Hoover, Address, December 7, 1961.)

"The Communist Party, USA, has been and is engaged in an all-out war against American freedom. Its tactics of confusion, retreat, advance, infiltration, and hypocrisy are in full play. The attack is both legal and illegal, offensive and defensive, open and concealed.

"Above the surface a gigantic propaganda and agitation campaign is in progress, a campaign that depends for success upon the support of non-communists." (Hoover, *Masters of Deceit*, p. 195.)

"Communists are committed to the destruction of our way of life and dedicated to the establishment of a world communist society. This conflict with communism is not a struggle of our choosing. But, even though we did not start it, we cannot ignore it. We must win the struggle if freedom is to survive." (Hoover, *A Study of Communism*, p. 18.)

Yes, "We are at war with this sinister conspiracy! Every communist today must be considered an enemy, wherever he may be, at home or abroad! A 'soft' approach toward the menace of communism can lead only to national disaster! . . ."

The communists are winning the war and building their empire largely with the help of non-communists—fellow travelers, sympathizers, dupes, liberals, etc.

Some people foolishly believe that the communists are changing, that they are "mellowing." This is not true.

"Today's headlines," says Hoover, "remind us there has been no basic change in communist imperialism. The danger which world communism presents to the free nations has not abated. If anything, it has increased." (Hoover, *A Study of Communism*, Foreword.)

"In our quest for peace, we must never lose sight of the well-documented fact that every Red leader from Marx and Engels through Khrushchev, Mao, and the American communist spokesman Gus Hall is dedicated to an ideology which upholds world conquest as its ultimate goal.

"The communists have never deviated from this objective." (Hoover, Address, November 16, 1963.)

The intellectuals, liberals, and dupes are so obsessed with the idea of "academic freedom" that they encourage the use of communist speakers in our colleges, at youth conventions, and even high schools. This is perversion of the true meaning of academic freedom.

Again J. Edgar Hoover warns us and expresses his fear in these words:

"I do fear so long as school boards and parents tolerate conditions whereby communists and fellow travelers under the guise of academic freedom can teach our youth a way of life that eventually will destroy the sanctity of the home, that undermines faith in God, that causes them to scorn respect for constituted authority and sabotage our revered Constitution." (Hoover, *Menace of Communism*, p. 11.)

"Today, the communists are engaged in an intensive campaign to control the minds and win the allegiance of American youth. . . . During the past two years, communist spokesmen have appeared on nearly 100 campuses from coast to coast. Their purpose: To create confusion, raise questions and spread doubt among our young people concerning the American way of life. . . ." They are setting a trap for the nation's youth.

In a masterful address, "Keys to Freedom," before the Catholic Youth Organization recently, J. Edgar Hoover issued shocking and timely warnings to complacent Americans.

"Today," he declared, "the communists are engaged in an intensive campaign to control the minds and win the allegiance of American youth. Toward this end, a National Youth Commission has been established within the Communist Party, USA; special publications have been issued; front groups have been organized; and an ambitious speech program has been directed against our colleges and universities.

"It is indeed ironic that Communist Party speakers—whose minds and thoughts and actions are in no manner free—should demand the opportunity to parrot the Moscow line to young Americans under the guise of academic freedom!

"Academic freedom is not an instrument for the perpetuation of conspiratorial ideologies. Nor is it an agent of self-destruction—a freedom to destroy freedom. As a free-flowing channel of truth and knowledge, academic freedom is not obligated to carry along the silted tributaries of lies and distortions of known communists.

"The communists look upon students as potential sympathizers, supporters and contributors to the party's cause. Nor are they unmindful of the rich opportunity for infiltration presented by unwary racial and nationality groups.

"This is especially true of the intense civil rights movement within the United States—for America's 20 million Negroes and the countless other citizens who share their objectives in the current struggle are a priority target for communist propaganda and exploitation. Every organization engaged in this struggle must constantly remain alert to this vital fact, for, once under communist domination, all freedoms and rights are lost."

One of the dangerous present-day fallacies is the idea that we can continue with a policy of "Peaceful Coexistence."

Here again Hoover warns us as follows:

"Key to the new Soviet strategy is the so-called 'peaceful coexistence' policy. It is a broad, psychological tactic cleverly devised by Khrushchev to serve a number of objectives. It is another powerful weapon in the communist arsenal of deception, a weapon concealed behind an alluring campaign designed to provide a cover for the goal of attaining a world-wide communist society through revolutionary means.

"Through the weapon of peaceful coexistence, Soviet communists are seeking to lull the free world—particularly the United States—into a false sense of security. It is a means of buying time through which they can consolidate past gains while probing for soft spots in the non-communist world which present opportunities for future expansion." (Hoover, *A Study of Communism*, p. 149.)

More is needed than merely to say that we oppose communism. We must aggressively take action to defeat it.

"It is the duty of all Americans to fully understand the true import of this threat to our heritage, to expose it, and to combat it with every weapon at our command." (Hoover, *Communist Target—Youth*, p. 11.)

"It is not enough to be against communism. We must shed our complacency and aggressively meet this challenge." (Hoover, Address, February 22, 1962.)

As the ward teaching message, July, 1961, stated:

"It is the duty of freedom loving people to oppose and resist this evil with all the strength God has given us. If we do not, we stand to lose all we and all our forebears have gained through the centuries."

What is needed is more patriotism—more real "super patriots" if you will.

"A free society," says Hoover, "depends for its vitality and strength upon the vigor and patriotism of its individual citizens." (Hoover, *A Study of Communism*, Foreword.)

"Today, perhaps as never before, America has need for doers of extraordinary deeds, men and women with the moral strength and courage of our forefathers. The smoldering embers of patriotism should be fanned into a flaming spirit of loyalty so that the whole world will know Americans will stand, fight, and die for the dignity of man." (F.B.I., *Law Enforcement Bulletin,* July, 1962.)

The real threat is here at home.

The seriousness of the insidious "internal" threat cannot be overemphasized.

Again Mr. Hoover warns:

"The communist threat from without must not blind us to the communist threat from within. The latter is reaching into the very heart of America through its espionage agents and a cunning, defiant, and lawless Communist Party, which is fanatically dedicated to the Marxist cause of world enslavement and destruction of the foundations of our Republic.

"The Communist Party in this country has attempted to infiltrate and subvert every segment of our society." (Hoover, Address, December 7, 1961.)

Unjust criticism of the anti-communists anti-socialists helps the conspiracy and is dangerous to our future.

J. Edgar Hoover, probably the best-informed man in America on the threatening conspiracy, has repeatedly warned us that the gravest danger we face today comes from the socialist-communist conspiracy—and from within.

Many people cannot see how this statement by Mr. Hoover can be true, since there are supposedly only about 10,000 or so party members in this country. Those who doubt Mr. Hoover overlook the fact that for every member of the communist conspiracy there are at least ten others willing and eager to do their bidding. In addition to this, the communists and their fellow travelers move toward key positions by which they can influence many others, just as iron filings move toward a magnet. Also, the communists, at this stage, do not themselves intend to do much of the actual close-in fighting. Instead, they make use of non-communists to serve their purposes. Their method of operation is to confuse the issues, divide one group against the other, and thus to conquer.

The communist method of confusing the issues is to use pseudo-idealistic and pseudo-moral words and phrases in order to trap the unwary into following their designs. The fisherman knows that he cannot entice a fish to bite upon a raw, steel hook, so he dresses it up with a nice, juicy worm and the poor fish bites. In the same way, the pseudo-moral and pseudo-idealistic expressions trap many innocents so that they will follow out the aims of the communist conspirators, for example, the false appeals made by the communists in the name of "peace" and the "brotherhood of man." They know full well that communism has nothing in common with these expressions as we understand them. Yet, they deliberately misuse them in order to deceive.

This has been the means by which the communists, throughout the world, have been able to set class against class, religion against religion, race against race and group against group. The conspiracy so enflames people against one another that they fight among themselves and thus bring about mutual destruction. The communists then come in and take over.

The present strength of the communist conspiracy by itself would be insufficient to accomplish their aims in this country. However, they are being given a tremendous push and able assistance by the Fabian socialists, their fellow travelers, dupes, liberals, etc. The name, Fabian, is derived from that of a Roman general who always avoided clear-cut contact with the enemy. Instead, he would whittle down the antagonist little by little, until the latter was so weakened that he would succumb.

The communists are eager to capitalize upon all areas of misunderstanding and unrest. Their cause is the cause of Soviet Russia, for the Communist Party, USA, is an inseparable part of the sinister international conspiracy which is financed and directed by the Kremlin. No amount of lies and duplicity can conceal this carefully documented fact.

If you want the terrifying facts about the communist use of the Negroes I recommend Manning Johnson's book, *Color, Communism, and Common Sense,* a reprint by *American Opinion Magazine* (Belmont 78, Massachusetts). The author, a Negro, was a communist for ten years and served on the national committee for the Communist Party here in America and assisted in planning the conspiracy against his own race.

Let me pause a moment to point out some pro-communist propaganda which has been widely circulated. It is frequently stated that communism is on the extreme left, and fascism is on the extreme right. This is absolutely false. It is true that communism is on the extreme left, but nazism and fascism are so closely allied with communism that J. Edgar Hoover has called communism, red fascism and nazism, black fascism. They are all forms of socialism. And, as has been pointed out by well-informed people in the West, they are all forms of *Governmentism* where the government becomes lord and master and we become serfs and slaves.

The extreme right wing is composed of the anarchists who believe that people are so good at heart that no government at all is needed. Our forefathers knew that, while most people try to do the right thing, there are a few who run amuck. They, therefore, established our great constitutional Republic—a government of limited powers. They believed that we must have some government but it must be bound down by the chains of our Constitution, so that it will not slip farther and farther over into the realm of *governmentism,* whether it be communism, nazism, fascism, welfare-statism or some other form of socialism.

Please note the words of George Washington, who stated:

"Government is not reason, it is not eloquence—it is force! Like fire, it is a dangerous servant and a fearful master!" And, at a later date, Woodrow Wilson said that "the history of liberty is the history of limitations of government power, not the increase if it." And at a still later day, that great spiritual leader and patriot, President David O. McKay said this: "During the first half of the twentieth century we have traveled far into the soul-destroying land of socialism." (Church News, *Deseret News,* March 14, 1953.)

Now I want to point out just a few of the ways in which America is tripping down the primrose path. Anyone who is interested and who would care to make a careful study of the subject, will be both amazed and shocked at the progress made by the Marxian Socialists. Their tremendous influence and power can be grasped if we will read the carefully documented book by Dan Smoot, a former FBI administrative supervisor and assistant to J. Edgar Hoover, entitled *The Invisible Government.* This book shows how the Fabians, operating through many influential organizations, have reached out their tentacles and are throttling free enterprise at the same time they are pyramiding and concentrating immense power in the Federal Government. In this way the advance of communism is being comforted, aided, and abetted by those who are not members of the communist conspiracy but who adhere to the same principles.

Dr. Carew Hunt, a world-wide authority on communist strategy, states: "Yet, where the ends they seek are concerned, Socialism and Communism are virtually interchangeable terms, as anyone who consults the 'Oxford English Dictionary' or any standard textbook will discover. . . . Indeed, Lenin's party continued to call itself

'Social Democrat' until the seventh Party Congress of March, 1918, when it substituted the term 'Bolshevik' as a protest against the non-revolutionary attitude of the socialist parties of the West."

President J. Reuben Clark, Jr., expressed his conviction on this point in these significant words:

"The paths we are following, if we move forward thereon will inevitably lead us to socialism or communism, and these two are as like as two peas in a pod in their ultimate effect upon our liberties.

"And never forget for one moment that communism and socialism are state slavery. World conquest has been, is now, and ever will be its ultimate goal."

The communists and fellow-travelers have never deviated from this objective. Despite the high-pressure campaign they have insidiously directed behind Khrushchev's phrase of "peaceful coexistence," the communists know that this is simply a propaganda slogan. It is devised to further their own ends by stirring the hopes and emotions of those who seek an end to the turmoil, fear, and sorrow that world communism itself created.

Actions continue to speak louder than words, and certainly the communists have shown no indication of a sincere quest for peace. Here are a few examples. There are many.

The take-over of Cuba and the establishment of a communist base and island fortress in America; the ever-constant infiltration of red fascists into countries of Central and South America to create a Sovietized Latin America; the increase of espionage activities by Soviet and satellite agents in our country, particularly those who strive to penetrate our government processes from the protection afforded them by diplomatic assignments in New York in the United Nations and in Washington; the frantic efforts of the Communist Party, USA, to subvert our youth; and the intense drive of the communists operating from concealed positions to wrest control of the movement for Negro rights—does all this indicate a real and sincere desire to live in "peaceful coexistence"?

To the socialist-communist conspiracy there is no such thing as "peaceful coexistence" except as a tool for further conquest. Their stated objective is to "bury" us.

Since about the time of Woodrow Wilson, Fabian socialists have been able to cuddle close to key people in our government and those who exercise influence. I will not take the time to trace their activities through the various administrations since Wilson's time. I will be content to give you two or three examples approximating that of the Fabian socialists.

Today, Walt Whitman Rostow, who is the chief planner for the State Department, has expressed a dangerous point of view somewhat like this: We must do everything in our power to avoid irritating and antagonizing the communists. They are, after all, merely rough and crude socialists and we must avoid doing anything that would escalate into a war. In fact, what we should do is to help them to develop so that they will mature and outgrow their violent impulses. In this way the communists will move somewhat over in our direction. At the same time we must move our country over toward the left with more and more socialism until, ultimately, the two will merge. Each country will then give up its armaments and armed forces and place them in the hands of a One-World Government. (See the book, *A Proposal: Key to an Effective Foreign Policy,* by Walt W. Rostow and Max F. Millikan, Harper, New York, 1957. An outgrowth of the Dartmouth Conference in the fall of 1960 and the Crimea Conference of May, 1961, was the pamphlet, *Freedom from War, the United States Program for General and Complete Disarmament in a Peaceful World,* U.S. State Department Publication No. 7277, Disarmament Series 5, released September, 1961, U.S. Government Printing Office.)

And Arthur Schlesinger, Jr., former professor of history
at Harvard and high in the councils of government, said:
"There seems no inherent obstacle to the gradual advance
of socialism in the United States through a series of New
Deals," and, that socialism appears quite practical as a long
time proposition.

In either case the whole tendency is toward more and
more *governmentism*, more and more centralization and less
and less individual responsibility and freedom.

An interesting example of the socialist mind at work is
the present so-called Civil Rights Bill of 1963. I am going to
quote, in part, from a talk made by John C. Satterfield, past
president of the American Bar Association, over the Manion
Forum, weekly broadcast No. 468, September 15, 1963:

"It is clothed in the name of civil rights and is called
the Civil Rights Act of 1963. As a matter of fact, it is 10
percent civil rights and it is 90 percent extension of Federal
executive power at the expense of individuals, states and
municipalities—in fact, at the expense of everyone. . . .

"Do you borrow money from a bank that is in the
Federal Deposit Insurance Corporation system or the
Federal Reserve system? Have you an FHA or VA loan?
Have you a Small Business Administration loan? Are you
a realtor, developer, home owner? Are you interested in
schools and colleges? Are you a farmer who has anything
to do with the Farm Credit Administration, Commodity
Credit Corporation, Soil Conservation Service, Federal Crop
Insurance, REA, Agricultural Research?

"If you are any of these, or participate in any of these,
then under this Act the Federal Fair Employment Practices
Commission will dictate to you whom you may hire, whom
you may fire, whom you promote, whom you demote, and
how you may handle your employees. . . .

"Not only that, but it brings in almost every profession
and every business—lawyers, realtors, doctors, small estab-
lishments, restaurants, gasoline stations, theaters, hotels,

motels and lodging houses—and the Federal control will never end. . . .

"Under the provisions of this Act, combining them all, the United States Commissioner of Education could come into a school and force the transfer of children from one school to another until there was either racial balance or religious balance. . . .

"Not only that, but the next step to a complete and uncontrolled dictatorship of any government is the control of the voting and of the electoral machinery. . . . This Act . . . would transfer from the states to the Federal Government the right to fix qualifications for voters, contrary to the provision of the Constitution of the United States. It would also transfer, under the circumstances stated in the Act, the right of registration of voters from the state and local officers to Federal referees. . . .

"You should think about this legislation because it destroys everything that we have heretofore felt protects us from a complete and absolute power of a central government. It is something that strikes home to every businessman, every home owner, and every worker in the United States. . . ."

In other words, we may say that the states would be reduced to little more than subdivisions within the central government and largely subject to its control. It would be almost certain to result in an all-powerful national government with authority to intervene in the private affairs of individual citizens. It would, furthermore, control and adjust relationships between men in accordance with the dictates of those in charge.

It has been truly said by our former Chief Executive, Dwight D. Eisenhower, that, "The federal government did not create the states of this Republic. The states created the federal government. . . . If the states lose their meaning, our entire system of government loses its meaning and the

next step is the rise of the centralized national state in which
the seeds of autocracy can take root and grow."

Those are strong but true words.

Never forget that history is filled with examples of men
who mean to be good rulers but who nevertheless mean
to rule.

With reference to the United Nations and spurious
appendages, I would like to quote the *International Security
Annual Report for 1956*, p. 213, as made by the Senate
Internal Security Sub-Committee, as follows: "What appears, on the surface at least, to be by far the worst danger
spot, from the standpoint of disloyal and subversive activity
among Americans employed by international organizations,
is UNESCO—the United Nations Educational, Scientific
and Cultural Organization. Among less than ninety Americans employed by UNESCO the International Organizations Employees Loyalty Board found fourteen cases of
doubtful loyalty." Then, in the footnote, we see this:
"Information in the possession of the sub-committee, indicat-
ing a great deal of evidence not yet publicly adduced, points
to the possibility that the parent body, the U.N., may be the
worst 'spot' of all." There is no indication that there has
been the slightest improvement in the United Nations or
its satellites since that time.

I have in my possession a copy of an unpublished manu-
script on the United Nations Charter prepared in 1945 and
given to me by that eminent international lawyer and former
Under Secretary of State, J. Reuben Clark, Jr.

President Clark's declarations on this, as on other subjects, emphasize more and more with the passing of time
his vision and statesmanship.

Commenting on the United Nations Charter and the
"travesty on exhaustive consideration" as the charter was
hastily approved by the Congress, under urging from the
State Department, he continues with a devastating analysis

and a sober warning to the American people that there will
be a day of reckoning. I believe that day is near at hand.
The hopes and the aspirations of the people have been
betrayed. I hope this scholarly, unpublished memorandum
by President Clark with its penetrating analysis will some-
day soon be available in full. Meantime, I urge all to read
the solid volume, *Stand Fast by the Constitution*, which
embodies much of J. Reuben Clark's timely instruction.
Meantime let us have no further blind devotion to the
communist-dominated United Nations.

Today it is becoming an increasing handicap, it seems,
to one's career in government for a man or woman to take
seriously his pledge of allegiance to our Constitution. Witness the firing of Mr. Otto F. Otepka, because he believed
in a higher service—that service to our nation comes above
service to any particular department of government.

The open and covert management of the news in this
country is another case, frightening in its implications. One
high government official has made the appalling statement
to the effect that it is all right for the government to lie to
the people if it serves the government's purpose to lie. Certainly lies can take place by omission as well as by
commission.

At this point I quote a statement by Virgil Jordan:
"In these days of fear and confusion, let us remember that
the endless repetition of a lie, or the multiplication of an
empty promise does not make a truth. Truth is something
more than the greatest common denominator of mass ignorance and greed. It is never determined or demonstrated
by the majorities or pluralities or popular error and appetite.
Ultimately, with God's aid, it always emerges and finally
prevails, supreme in its power over the destiny of mankind,
and terrible in its retribution for those who deny, defy, or
betray it."

Constantine Brown, in an article in a recent issue of
the *Congressional Record*, told of prominent people who had

defected from communism who now fear they have joined the losing side.

They gave two reasons:

1. Communism will win because western leaders (particularly in the United States) do not want to believe that the Soviets are planning to conquer the world.

2. Khrushchev knows that the United States will offer only token opposition to the Soviets' plans to conquer in Latin America.

Now the question arises—what can we do to preserve our Constitution, and how can we avoid being misled into doing those things that would actually help to destroy it? During last October conference I spoke on the subject "Be Not Deceived." I said there were three keys one could use to avoid deception: first, the scriptures; second, the words of prophets, especially the President of the Church (particularly the living one); and, third, the Holy Ghost.

The scriptures tell us about the war in heaven over free agency—similar to the war we are going through now, where the devil's program was guaranteed security as opposed to the Lord's program of letting each choose for himself even if he makes the wrong choice. Once you understand these scriptures you will understand why the Presidents of the Church have opposed communism, socialism, and the welfare state and you will see why you must oppose them, too, if you are in harmony with the word of the Lord. The scriptures also tell about our inspired Constitution. If you accept these scriptures, you will automatically reject the counsel of men like Senator Fulbright and others who depreciate our Constitution. If you use the scriptures as a guide you know what the Book of Mormon has to say regarding murderous conspiracies in the last day and how we are to awake to our awful situation today. I find certain elements in the Church do not like to read the Book of Mormon and Doctrine and Covenants so much—they have too much to say about freedom.

The second criterion is the prophets, especially the living President. Do you realize what President McKay has said about some recent decisions of our Supreme Court? Do you realize that he has called communism the greatest threat to the Church today and has said that this country has traveled far into the soul-destroying land of socialism? He has opposed programs of federal aid to education; he has supported right-to-work laws. Are you in harmony with the prophet's declarations? If you accept the scriptures and the prophets, then you will automatically separate yourself from the philosophy of some Mormons, and you will have to part a with a number of our national leaders and their programs.

The last criterion is the Holy Ghost—the test of the Spirit. You cannot use this test unless you have the Spirit of the Lord with you and that only comes through righteous living—which means being in harmony with Church doctrine in addition to simply being active in Church work and attending meetings.

These are the three main keys—apply them and you will avoid pitfalls and traps which even members of the Church and some teachers may set for you. President Joseph F. Smith said that one of the three things that plagued the Church within was false educational ideas—and I am sure you will be introduced to some of these ideas somewhere along your path. Using the scriptures and the prophets and the Spirit as a guide, we can eliminate many of the deceptions and false philosophies and cure-alls of men and discern between the wheat and the chaff.

Thus, with the scriptures and the words of the prophets for a guide line, it is easier to select our reading—for we need information out of the best books to help us in this fight for our freedom. And when it comes to the writings of men, in addition to the tests we have suggested, it is helpful to select the men who have proved most accurate over the years. On this basis may I give to you my own personal recommendation of some reading which will help you in the fight to save our Constitution.

First, for a number of years President J. Reuben Clark, Jr., served on the board of trustees of the Foundation for Economic Education while he was a member of the First Presidency. President Clark, as you probably know, was an Under Secretary of State and Ambassador to Mexico. He wrote the famous memorandum on the Monroe Doctrine. In 1923 in the Salt Lake Tabernacle he warned us of the communist-socialist menace and what it was going to do— and he was right. No one in the Church has shown greater insight regarding our Constitution and the socialist-communist threat to it. The Foundation for Economic Education with which he served puts out some of the most enlightening freedom literature available. They also put out a free monthly magazine, entitled *The Freeman*, which is excellent. They will be happy to send you a free catalog of their literature. May I mention some of the books which they distribute: *The Federalist*, written by Alexander Hamilton, John Jay, and James Madison, three of our inspired founding fathers, explaining why the need of a constitution; *The Constitution of the United States*, by Mussatti; *The Clichés of Socialism; The Mainspring of Human Progress*, by Weaver; *Economics in One Lesson*, by Hazlitt; and *The Admiral's Log*, by Admiral Ben Moreell, which book is also on the MIA reading list. The address for the Foundation for Economic Education is simply Irvington-on-Hudson, New York.

These books and others will show you what America stands for—our free enterprise system—our constitutional republic—how we became the world's greatest power. For first you need to know what America stands for before you can realize what could be a threat to it. As President

McKay has said, the fostering of full economic freedom lies at the base of all our liberties.

The next thing we must know about is the major enemy to our way of life—socialistic-communism. In October conference, 1959, President McKay admonished us to read what he called an excellent book, *The Naked Communist*. I agree with the President of the Church. Probably no man in America knows the internal communist threat better than J. Edgar Hoover—his two books on communism should be *must* reading. They are *Masters of Deceit,* and *A Study of Communism. You Can Trust the Communists,* by Dr. Fred Schwarz, whom President McKay called a true friend of freedom, is also an enlightening book. The House Committee on Un-American Activities and the Senate Internal Security Subcommittee have both put out instructive information. A list of their publications is available free of charge from the U.S. Superintendent of Documents, Washington 25, D.C.

Once you get the facts about our American constitutional republic and the threats to it—then you are going to want to do something. Certainly those who are organized and have a plan and are dedicated, though they be few, will always defeat the many who are not organized and have no plan of dedication. The communists have proved this, and the fighters for freedom must realize it too. If, then, you want to have impact through an organization, make sure that organization squares with the scriptures and the prophets and the spirit. Then move forward and use your free agency to accomplish that which is virtuous and praiseworthy and let the devil and his agents and dupes howl.

Yes, the Fabian socialists are as busy as bees rolling out the red carpet which leads inevitably to communism. Faced with this situation our first duty is that of education. Starting with ourselves we must become familiar with the broad outlines of the movement toward destruction. We must, as President McKay has urged, become alerted and informed.

After becoming informed ourselves, we must carry the word to all within hearing or seeing range, so that they, too, can become awakened. Take every opportunity to pass sound literature and books around so that your neighbors and their neighbors will awaken before it is too late. We are literally in a race against time, and we must take every opportunity to spread the word.

We must not become confused over side issues. Our enemy is not the Catholic, not the Protestant, not the Negro, not the white man, not the Jew, not the gentile, not employers, not employees, not the wealthy, not the poor, not the worker, and not the employer. Our mortal enemies are the Satanic communists and those who prepare the path for them.

It is not, however, enough to be acquainted with the grave dangers facing these United States. We must also instruct ourselves, and others, in the great spiritual values underlying our divinely inspired Constitution and our American free-enterprise system. One of the many sure ways of defeating our enemy is to instruct the people about the eternal verities of our own country. A mind, so enlightened, will reject Marxian socialism whether it be in the form of communism, nazism, fascism, welfare-statism or some other man-made monstrosity.

In this time of deadly peril we must choose men and women to represent us in our government who have attained an inner atunement of mind, heart and soul with God. Only these people have anchors firmly rooted and strong enough to withstand the slings and arrows of outrageous fortune. They, only, have the inner sense of direction, stability of spirit and firmness of character essential to our survival.

We must not place in positions of trust cheap opportunists who will sell their souls for a mess of pottage. Rather we should place in public office men and women who place the love of God first in their lives and who, as a consequence, can serve their fellow men with true wisdom.

Not cheap politicians but statesmen are needed today. Not opportunists but men and women of principle must be demanded by the people. In this time of great stress and danger we must place only those dedicated to the preservation of our Constitution, our American Republic, and responsible freedom under God. "Oh, God, give us men with a mandate higher than the ballot box."

In closing let me quote Bishop Exeter:

> Give us men
> Strong and stalwart ones;
> Men whom highest hope inspires,
> Men whom purest honor fires,
> Men who trample Self beneath them,
> Men who made their country wreath them
> > As her noble sons,
> Men who never shame their mothers,
> Men who never fail their brothers
> True, however false are others:
> > Give us men—I say again
> > Give us Men!
>
> Give us Men!
> Men who, when the tempest gathers,
> Grasp the standards of their fathers
> > In the thickest fight:
> Men who strike for home and altar,
> > (Let the coward cringe and falter)
> > God defend the right:
> True as truth though lorn and lonely
> Tender, as the brave are only:
> Men who tread where saints have trod,
> Men for Country—Home—and God:
> > Give us Men: I say again—again—
> > Give us such Men!

(*Brigham Young University, Provo, Utah*, December 10, 1963.)

A Nation Asleep

I thank God for freedom—the right of choice. I am grateful for this great nation. Every true Latter-day Saint throughout the world loves the USA. The Constitution of this land is part of every Latter-day Saint's religious faith.

This is not just another nation, not just a member of a family of nations. This is a great and glorious nation with a divine mission and a prophetic history and future. It has been brought into being under the inspiration of heaven.

It is our firm belief that the Constitution of this land was established by men whom the God of heaven raised up unto that very purpose. It is our conviction also, that the God of heaven guided the founding fathers in establishing it for his particular purpose.

The founders of this republic were deeply spiritual men. They believed men are capable of self-government and that it is the job of government to protect freedom and foster private initiative.

Our earliest American fathers came here with a common objective—freedom of worship and liberty of conscience.

They were familiar with the sacred scriptures, and they believed that liberty is a gift of heaven. To them, man as a child of God emphasized the sacredness of the individual and the interest of a kind Providence in the affairs of men and nations.

These leaders recognized the need for divine guidance and the importance of vital religion and morality in the affairs of men and nations.

To the peoples who should inhabit this blessed land of the Americas, the Western Hemisphere, an ancient prophet uttered this significant promise and solemn warning:

"Behold this is a choice land, and whatsoever nation

shall possess it shall be free from bondage, and from captivity and from all other nations under heaven, if they will but serve the God of the land, who is Jesus Christ. . . . For behold, this is a land which is choice above all other lands; wherefore he that doth possess it shall serve God or shall be swept off; for it is the everlasting decree of God." (See Ether 2.)

Ancient American prophets 600 years before Christ, foresaw the coming of Columbus and those who followed. These prophets saw the establishment of the colonies, the War for Independence and predicted the outcome.

These prophecies are contained in a volume of scripture called the Book of Mormon. This sacred record, a companion volume to the Holy Bible which it confirms, is an added witness to the divine mission of Jesus as the Son of God and Redeemer of the world.

How I wish every American and every living soul would read the Book of Mormon. I testify to you that it is true. It tells about the prophetic history and mission of America. It gives the comforting assurance that God has kept this great nation—as it were—in the hollow of his hand in preparation for its great mission.

Yes, the Lord planned it all. Why? In preparation for the opening of a new gospel dispensation—the last and greatest of all dispensations in preparation for the second coming of the Lord, Jesus Christ. To achieve his purposes the Lord had to have a base of operations. Later he revealed to a modern prophet that the Constitution of this land was established by "wise men" whom the Lord "raised up unto this very purpose." The Lord also directed that the constitutional laws of the land supporting the principle of freedom, should be upheld and that honest and wise men should be sought for and upheld in public office.

The establishment of this great Christian nation with a spiritual foundation was all in preparation for the restoration of the gospel following the long night of apostasy. Then, in 1820, the time had arrived. God the Father and his Son Jesus Christ made their glorious appearance. I give you a few words from the Prophet Joseph Smith who was the instrument in God's hands in restoring the gospel and establishing the true Church of Christ again upon the earth. In response to humble prayer Joseph relates: "I saw a pillar of light exactly over my head, above the brightness of the sun, which descended gradually until it fell upon me. . . . When the light rested upon me I saw two Personages, whose brightness and glory defy all description, standing above me in the air. One of them spake unto me, calling me by name and said, pointing to the other—This is My Beloved Son. Hear Him!" (Joseph Smith 2:16-17.)

To me this is the greatest event that has occurred in this world since the resurrection of the Master—and it happened in America.

Later other heavenly messengers came to restore the authority of the Holy Priesthood and important keys essential to the opening of the final gospel dispensation. The Church was organized in 1830. Immediately, in response to divine command, missionary-messengers began to carry the important message of salvation throughout the world. It is a world message intended for all of God's children.

And so when this nation was established—the Church was restored and from here the message of the restored gospel has gone forth. All according to divine plan!

This then becomes the Lord's base of operations in these latter days. And this base will not be shifted out of its place—the land of America. This nation will, in a measure at least, fulfil its mission even though it may face serious and troublesome days. The degree to which it achieves its full mission depends upon the righteousness of its people. God, through his power has established a free people in this land as a means of helping to carry forward his purposes.

"It was his latter-day purpose to bring forth his gospel in America, not in any other place. It was in America where the Book of Mormon plates were deposited. That was no accident. It was his design. It was in this same America where they were brought to light by angelic ministry. It was" . . . here "where he organized his modern Church, where he, himself made a modern personal appearance."

It was here under a free government and a strong nation that protection was provided for his restored Church.

Now God will not permit America, his base of operations, to be destroyed. He has promised protection to this land if we will but serve the God of the land. He has also promised protection to the righteous even, if necessary, to send fire from heaven to destroy their enemies. (I Nephi 22.)

No, God's base of operations will not be destroyed. But it may be weakened and made less effective. One of the first rules of war strategy—and we are at war with the adversary and his agents—is to protect the base of operations. This we must do if we are to build up the kingdom throughout the world and safeguard our God-given freedom.

How will we protect this base of operations?

We must protect this base of operations from every threat—from sin, from unrighteousness, immorality, from desecration of the Sabbath day, from lawlessness, from parental and juvenile delinquency.

We must protect it from dirty movies, filthy advertising, from salacious and suggestive TV programs, magazines, and books.

We must protect this base from idleness, subsidies, doles, and soft governmental paternalism which weakens initiative, discourages industry, destroys character, and demoralizes the people.

We must protect this American base from the brainwashing, increasingly administered to our youth in many educational institutions across the land, by some misinformed instructors and some wolves in sheep's clothing. Their false indoctrination, often perpetrated behind the front of so-called academic freedom, is leaving behind many faithless students, socialist-oriented, who are easy subjects for state tyranny.

The only threat to the liberty and independence of the American people from abroad is the threat of world communism spreading from its base in the Soviet Union.

But the best authorities are confident that the Soviets will not provoke a major war. Their economy would not support it.

Lenin said, "The soundest strategy in war is to postpone operations until the moral disintegration of the enemy renders the mortal blow possible and easy."

We are afraid to live righteously according to eternal principles—economic, moral and spiritual. This is our danger.

We must never forget that nations may—and usually do—sow the seeds of their own destruction while enjoying unprecedented prosperity.

As Jenkin Lloyd Jones said, "It is time we hit the sawdust trail. It is time we revived the idea that there is such a thing as sin—just plain old willful sin. It is time we brought self-discipline back into style. . . .

"Let's blow the whistle on plays that bring blushes— . . . Let's not be awed by movie characters with barnyard morals even if some of them have been photographed climbing aboard the presidential yacht. Let us pay more attention in our news columns to the decent people everywhere who are trying to do something for the good of others.

"In short, let's cover up the cesspool and start planting some flowers.

"I am fed up with the educationists and pseudo-scientists who have under-rated our potential as people. . . . I am tired of seeing America debased and low-rated in the eyes of foreigners. I am genuinely disturbed that to idealistic youth in many countries the fraud of communism appears synonymous with morality, while we, the chief repository of real freedom, are regarded as being in the last stages of decay.

"In this hour of fear, confusion and self-doubt . . . let there be a fresh breeze, a breeze of new honesty, new idealism, new integrity."

To protect this base we must protect the soul of America—we must return to a love and respect for the basic spiritual concepts upon which this nation has been established. We must study the Constitution and the writings of the founding fathers.

Yes, we must protect the Lord's base of operations by moving from unsound economic policies which encourage creeping socialism and its companion, insidious, atheistic communism.

If we are to protect this American base we must realize that all things, including information disseminated by our schools, churches, and government, should be judged according to the words of the prophets, especially the living prophet. This procedure coupled with the understanding which will come through the Spirit of the Lord, if we are living in compliance with the scriptures, is the only sure foundation and basis of judgment. Any other course of action leaves us muddled, despondent, wandering in shades of gray, easy targets for Satan.

If we fail in these pressing and important matters we may well fall far short of the great mission the Lord has proffered and outlined for America and for his divinely restored Church.

Yes, this is a choice land—a nation with a prophetic history.

God bless America and all the free world. And may God protect his latter-day base of operation that his glorious message of salvation may go forth to all the world.

(*Tabernacle, Salt Lake City, Utah, April Conference, 1962.*)

It Cannot Happen Here

The late Henry Grady Weaver of Georgia, who at the time of his death was an official of General Motors, stated in his stimulating book, *The Mainspring of Human Progress* that human *liberty* is the mainspring of human progress. He further proclaimed that progress comes through the "effective use of our individual energies, personal initiatives and imaginative abilities—applied to the things and forces of nature," in an atmosphere of *liberty*, under the blessings of God.

The one great revolution in the world today is the revolution for human *liberty*. This was the paramount issue we all faced in the great council in heaven before this earth life. It has been the issue throughout the ages. It is the issue today.

It is difficult for Americans to understand the danger to our *liberty*. "It is generally outside the range of our experience."

But we live today in an age of peril. We are threatened with the loss not only of material wealth but of something far more precious—our liberty itself.

Never before in the history of our country has there been a greater need for all of our people to take time to discover what is happening in the world. Every day decisions are being made affecting the lives of millions of human beings.

We as a people have never known bondage. *Liberty* has always been our blessed lot. Few of us have ever seen people who have lost their freedom—their *liberty*. And when reminded of the danger of losing our *liberty* and independence our attitude has usually been—*It cannot happen here*.

We must never forget that nations may—and they

usually do—sow the seeds of their own destruction while enjoying unprecedented prosperity.

The children of Israel were willing to sacrifice liberty and wanted Moses to be their king. Generations later their descendants begged Samuel the Prophet to give them a king. He pointed out the fallacy of their reasoning.

Samuel, like other great spiritual leaders both ancient and modern, saw the results that would follow the surrender of liberty.

In that sacred volume of scripture, The Book of Mormon, we note the great and prolonged struggle for *liberty*. We also note the complacency of the people and their frequent willingness to give up their liberty for the promises of a would-be provider.

The record reveals that men "of cunning device . . . and . . . many flattering words," . . . sought . . . "to destroy the foundation of *liberty* which God had granted unto them. . . ."

Then Moroni, the chief commander of the armies . . . dramatically rent his coat; and he took a piece thereof, and wrote upon it—"In memory of our God, our religion, and freedom, and our peace, our wives, and our children"— and he fastened it upon the end of a pole. . . . (and he called it the title of *liberty*) and he bowed himself to the earth, and he prayed mightily unto his God for the blessings of *liberty*, to rest upon his brethren. . . ." (Alma 46.)

This great general Moroni, like the prophets whose words are recorded in The Book of Mormon, spoke of the Americas as a chosen land—the land of *liberty*. He led the people in battle who were willing to fight to "maintain their *liberty*."

And the record states:

". . . that he caused the title of *liberty* to be hoisted upon every tower which was in all the land . . . and thus Moroni planted the standard of *liberty* among the Nephites." (*Ibid.*, 46:36.)

This is our need today—to plant the standard of *liberty* among our people throughout the Americas.

While this incident occurred some seventy years before Christ, the struggle continued through one thousand years as covered by this sacred Book of Mormon record. In fact, the struggle for *liberty* is a continuing one—it is with us in a very real sense today right here on this choice land of the Americas. Yes, on an island strategically situated only ninety miles from our shores.

Just a short time ago Fidel Castro broadcast to the world his boastful confession that he had been a hard-core communist all of his adult life. He gloried in the fact that he had been able to confuse and deceive many people simply by saying he was not a communist. And because there were gullible people in this country and other countries who believed his false assertions he was able to establish a Soviet beachhead—"A Communist satellite under active Russian control."

Americans must face the cold hard fact that Fidel Castro was encouraged and supported in his seizure of Cuba. Why? Simply because many Americans were led to believe the falsehood that he would resist Soviet influence and restore the full basic *liberty* of the Cuban people. A few of us issued early warnings based on unimpeachable evidence. Two United States ambassadors repeatedly warned that Castro was part of the communist conspiracy and that he was working for the communist conquest of Cuba. These voices went unheeded.

This is merely a repetition of the same deceitful pattern which was used after World War II to have us tolerate revolutionary communists in China—to accept them as "agrarian reformers" and allow them to seize and enslave some 450,000,000 people on the Chinese mainland.

This is the same deceitful pattern which we have been asked to accept in the Congo, in Laos, in British Guiana, etc. In fact, everywhere the communist conspiratorial machinery is preparing for a seizure of power, we are assured there is no immediate danger from communism.

In less than half a century this evil system has gained control over one-third of mankind, and it is steadily pursuing its vicious goal of control over all the rest of the world. It is time—and past time—for us to be alarmed.

I raised a voice of warning two years ago (1960) upon my return from South America. The good people of Latin America do not believe that suppression is the road to freedom. Today Cuba is being used as a base to spread subversion and armed revolution throughout Latin America. Cuba is being used as a funnel through which communists are infiltering other American republics. There can be no stability in Latin America as long as Cuba is communist controlled, or as long as "the shadow of the hammer and sickle is darkening the Western Hemisphere." The communist objective is to isolate North America.

Less than fifteen years ago communism was not a powerful force in Latin America. Today it is not only strongly present there as an enemy to be reckoned with—it is openly allied with a government located on an island only about ninety miles south of Key West, Florida.

The only political party now functioning in Cuba is the popular Socialist Party—the Communist Party under another name.

It is authoritatively reported that by the end of 1958 there were 316 known communist or pro-communist publications in Latin America, the largest numbers being fifty-five in Mexico. About one-half of these are newspapers and other periodicals. There were more than 150 communist publishing houses and bookstores. These activities have increased sharply since 1958.

(*South Wind Red* by Ray, p. 17.)

True to communist and dictator tradition, the Cuban government has deprived its people of the rights of a free press, free elections, and the protection of other fundamental human rights.

How did this situation come about? How is it possible for communism to be here now and moving into Africa, pressing upon all of Asia, threatening the Middle East, and increasingly becoming a danger in the western hemisphere?

There are, of course, many reasons. Our apathy—our complacent indifference is a major cause. Today, in America, we are living in a fool's paradise. We have permitted ourselves to be pacified and lulled away into carnal security as the Book of Mormon prophets predicted.

It was emphasized from this pulpit two years ago (1960) that we have a rich history to guide us. Think back with me a moment to the year 1823. In that year, James Monroe of Virginia was President. John Quincy Adams of Massachusetts was Secretary of State. These two men formed and announced a policy—the Monroe Doctrine—which has profoundly influenced the development of our entire hemisphere. The situation that precipitated this policy—known as the Monroe Doctrine—is as follows:

Several of the Latin American Republics had by force of arms recently won their independence from Spain and Portugal. Among them were Colombia, Mexico, Chile and Brazil.

Meanwhile, a number of the sovereign powers of Europe were seeking to enforce the "divine right of kings" with the express purpose of putting "an end to the system of representative government. . . ."

Our government refused to allow this. It said so very plainly in the celebrated Monroe Doctrine. The heart of the Monroe Doctrine consisted of these words: ". . . the American continents, by the free and independent condition which they have assumed and maintain, are henceforth not to be considered as subjects for future colonization by any European powers. . . ." The Monroe Doctrine, which should be, and is, an enduring cornerstone and living principle of national policy, stated further:

"The political system of the allied powers is essentially different . . . from that of AMERICA. . . ."

Surely if it were true a century and a half ago that European monarchy was essentially different from our American system of representative government, it is even more true today. The communist system is totally different, totally incompatible, totally inimical to our free way of life.

This is a time for decision. Further vacillation will serve only to drive all of Latin America straight into communist hands. If action is not taken against the power-drunken bandit and his cohorts, the day will soon come when it cannot be done at all.

The Monroe Doctrine was first invoked against the Russian Czar Alexander. The Cuban menace represents the first time in 100 years that a hostile foreign power has established a firm beachhead in the Americas.

The American people are deeply upset, frustrated and angry at what they fear is a retreat from the time-honored Monroe Doctrine—a retreat which could now end in war.

President J. Reuben Clark, Jr. whose scholarly work on the Monroe Doctrine as Under Secretary of State is well known—in tracing our destiny said the following:

"Then came our great Monroe Doctrine which placed us of the United States squarely behind efforts of Latin America to gain freedom and against those European states who would thwart it.

"God again moved us forward towards the destiny He has planned for us. He was preserving the blessings He had given to us." (Memorandum on the Monroe Doctrine, Dept. of State Publication #37, December 17, 1928.)

President Joseph Fielding Smith in his ever-timely volume, *The Progress of Man,* discusses America's fortifica-

tion against other nations and makes this significant
statement:

"The greatest and most powerful fortification in America is the Monroe Doctrine. . . . It appears to the casual
observer that this doctrine came by chance . . . but this
is not so. It was the inspiration of the Almighty which
rested upon John Quincy Adams, Thomas Jefferson and
other statesmen, and which finally found authoritative
expression in the message of President James Monroe to
Congress in the year 1823. . . .

"It is generally understood . . . in the Church that the
greatest and most significant principle by which this land
is fortified against the encroachments and invasions of European and Asiatic powers is found in the Monroe Doctrine. . . ." (Pages 357, 466, 467.)

This Monroe Doctrine was widely accepted by the
republics of the South and has been the continuing policy
of our Nation for almost a century and a half. It has been
reaffirmed by many American Presidents. We are on solid
traditional American ground in demanding that the communists should not attempt to extend their political system
to this side of the Atlantic Ocean.

In recent years the principles of the Monroe Doctrine
have been strengthened by various joint agreements among
the American nations. These should be invoked. The
longer we wait the more difficult the job will be.

It is almost unthinkable that any people would knowingly and wilfully take on themselves the yoke of communist
oppression. No nation has ever done so yet. If large masses
of the Cuban people have done so, it is because they have
been duped or coerced.

As a people who have known only *liberty* we are in-
clined to feel it cannot happen here. We have become
lulled away into a false security.

A most brilliant discussion of the Latin America problem appeared in the May 1961 issue of *American Opinion* and concluded with these words:

"... history gives us one more chance. If the American people are too blind or too cowardly to take that chance, then, whether or not we as individuals deserve it, you and I and all that we hold dear ... must suffer the doom that history mercilessly imposes on fools."

Why are we so timid in standing up to a godless communist police state which can't even feed its own people and whose economy will not support a major war? They "lead from weakness and we retreat from strength."

I say to you it *can* happen here. It *is* happening here. We have retreated from the Monroe Doctrine. Our liberty is in danger. But we go blithely and gullibly on our way. Some of us fall for the Kremlin line as planned by the mass murderer Khrushchev and call patriots "extremists" and accuse courageous liberty-loving citizens of "dividing our people."

As President David O. McKay said at the close of the last April general conference, quoting J. Edgar Hoover, "There is no place here in America for part-time patriots. This nation is face to face with the greatest danger ever to confront it, a sinister and deadly conspiracy which can be conquered only by an alert, informed citizenry. It is indeed appalling that some members of our society continue to deplore and criticize those who stress the Communist danger. Public indifference to this threat is tantamount to national suicide. Lethargy leads only to disaster...."

We must be vigilant. Let us unite. Let us join in our fight against the forces of anti-Christ.

Forgive me for being so blunt, but I feel most deeply on these matters. Possibly it is because I've seen at close range in the past few years much of this godless, treacherous conspiracy in more than forty different nations.

I realize that the bearer of bad news is always unpopular. As a people we love sweetness and light—especially sweetness. Ralph Waldo Emerson said that every mind must make a choice between truth and repose. Those who will learn nothing from history are condemned to repeat it. This we are doing in the Americas today.

As a Church we have a world message of salvation to deliver to our Father's children. The restored gospel can only thrive in an atmosphere of *liberty*. We are in a world-wide conflict. It is the first of its kind in history. It is between light and darkness; between *liberty* and slavery. It is a struggle for the souls of men. We must win this war.

In 1946 I stood in Czechoslovakia. The deadening socialist-communist philosophies were even then infiltrating that lovely country. Our church mission was thriving among these *liberty*-loving people. They too said it could not happen there. Only two years later it did happen—they had lost their *liberty*.

At the close of World War II I was serving as European Mission President and I visited Stanislaw M. Mikolajczyk in Warsaw. He was the leader of the liberty-loving Polish people and former Premier of the Polish government-in-exile. I had hoped we might do missionary work in Poland. Though Mikolajczyk was the leader of the indisputable majority of the electorate, he had to flee from Poland to save his life from the insidious encroaching communist police state.

I also talked to our Polish Ambassador, Arthur Bliss Lane. He told me of the tragic course of appeasement our government was pursuing in selling out the Polish people to the communists. Finally, because he was unable to endure it any longer, Lane voluntarily resigned so he could tell the story. He titled his book, *I Saw Poland Betrayed.*

And so the pattern has been repeated in country after country.

Rather than impede communism our policies in their

total effect have apparently helped promote it. The honest in heart, many of whom have probably already been murdered are deprived of the message of the restored gospel— good people who would have responded to the words of truth from our missionaries.

Who then is to blame? What then can be done?

To some extent we Latter-day Saints and Americans everywhere must share some blame for we have not been awake to the warnings of the prophets. We have not exerted our righteous influence as citizens to stop this disastrous course. Our skirts are not entirely clean. Many of us have been asleep in Zion— the Western Hemisphere.

But some say, "Why should we be so concerned? After all, if the Lord wants them to get the gospel message they'll get it."

We know if the Lord desired, he could preach the gospel this very instant to every soul and do all of our genealogical work. He could also right every wrong, feed the famished, plant our crops, train our children, etc. But his doctrine requires us to do our best ourselves in these areas and ask the Lord's help in our endeavors. After we've done all we can, then the Lord will cover for us.

Now what can be done? We have missionaries and Saints in South America. Those countries fall within the scope of the Monroe Doctrine. These countries are now being pushed in the direction of bondage—the loss of *liberty*.

What can we do to help meet this grave challenge from a godless, atheistic, cruelly materialistic system in order to preserve our God-given liberty?

We can encourage our government—wherever we live —to stand firm at all costs against any further expansion of despotic communism.

We can support our government in keeping the flame of *liberty* burning in the souls of the oppressed—wherever they may be throughout the world.

We can heed the words of men like Edward Hunter who

for twenty years has been reporting communist conspiracy and brain-washing from abroad and who recently wrote this:

"In Washington these days one hears a great deal of the word *escalation* but never the word *honor*.

"*Escalation* was the reason Americans had to stand by and watch with folded hands as a young man bled to death a hundred feet from them at the Berlin Wall of Shame, although we had every right to go in and stem his bleeding under wartime agreement.

"Imagine anyone telling an American only a few years back, that we would stand by idly, witnessing a man die needlessly because he wanted to be free! . . .

"*Escalation* is why we stood by wringing our hands when the East Germans started building the Wall, whereas as is now known, their orders were to stop if we showed any serious resistance.

"*Escalation,* if continued, will complete our softening-up, until we 'bury ourselves,' as Khrushchev predicts. . . .

"This soft *escalation* policy in Cuba, starting in 1958, permitted 'a small band of hoodlums, under the leadership of Fidel Castro' to conduct 'open warfare against the established government of Cuba, which was friendly towards the United States. . . .' We have, thus passed the time for soft and easy action to protect ourselves. We have only one course of action left: to destroy Communist power in Cuba by force of arms."

As I visited among the good people of Cuba in 1955 I had a secret hope we would soon be able to bring them the truths of the restored gospel. What are our prospects now? People said in Cuba in 1955: It cannot happen here. *We love liberty.*

The insidious but rapid take-over of Latin America is drawing ever closer to the final show-down.

Unless godless communism is stamped out of Cuba it

is only a matter of time until, like Czechoslovakia, other missions will likely close and more of our Father's children will be deprived of their liberty and the fulness of the everlasting gospel.

The message of salvation *must move* forward. God grant that every effort to stay its growth will be frustrated.

Courage and statesmanship are imperatively needed today. We must take chances for liberty. May God bless our national leaders in this time of crisis.

Yes, the effective preaching of the gospel can only thrive in an atmosphere of *liberty*.

Yes, we all say, we love *liberty*. But that is not enough. We must protect and safeguard that which we love. We must save *liberty*.

God grant us the wisdom and the courage so to do, before it is too late.

(*Tabernacle, Salt Lake City, Utah, October Conference,* 1962.)

Righteousness Exalteth a Nation

"Righteousness exalteth a nation." (Proverbs 14:34.) This statement of eternal truth from Proverbs appeared on the flyleaf and the last page of a booklet, at each plate at the President's Prayer Breakfast, in the Grand Ballroom of the Mayflower Hotel, February 7, 1963 in Washington, D. C. This annual breakfast is sponsored jointly by the U.S. Senate and House of Representatives Prayer Breakfast Groups and the International Christian Leadership Conference.

As I listened to the prayers, readings from the Old and New Testaments, and messages from government and non-government leaders, I reviewed hurriedly our spiritual background as a nation and today's spiritual needs.

For, truly, "Righteousness exalteth a nation; but sin is a reproach to any people."

The beautiful old print which hangs in Carpenter's Hall, Philadelphia, came to mind. It is captioned "The First Prayer in Congress, September 1774." It depicts most of the members of that Congress on their knees with our first President as leader.

I recalled the terrible winter at Valley Forge, and General George Washington on his knees in the snow, praying for divine aid. I thought of the words of Lincoln during another time of crisis as he said humbly:

"I have been driven many times to my knees by the overwhelming conviction that I had nowhere else to go."

George Washington acknowledged God's direction and stated:

"Of all the dispositions and habits which lead to political prosperity, religion and morality are indispensable supports. . . . Reason and experience both forbid us to expect that national morality can prevail in exclusion of religious principle." (Washington's Farewell Address.)

Lincoln knew that God rules in the affairs of men and nations. He solemnly declared:

"God rules this world—It is the duty of nations as well as men to own their dependence upon the overruling power of God, to confess their sins and transgressions in humble sorrow . . . and to recognize the sublime truth that those nations only are blessed whose God is the Lord."

The founding fathers knew that "where the spirit of the Lord is, there is liberty." (2 Cor. 3:17.)

The United States of America began and lives as a result of faith in God.

The Bible has been and is the foundation for this faith. . . .

"It is impossible to govern the world without the Bible," said George Washington.

The fathers of our country had to turn to religion in order that their new experiment make sense.

As I left the Prayer Breakfast, bidding good-bye to many warm friends, I thought of the greatness of America—the world's greatest power. During World War II she out-produced both her enemies and allies—"The American Miracle."

But I also recalled the latest FBI reports revealing the ever-increasing crime record—over seventeen percent increase in the nation's capital in 1962 alone. I recalled our shockingly defiant record of drunkenness and immorality and the fact we have become a nation of pleasure-seeking Sabbath breakers.

My thoughts turned to our homes and families—our ever-increasing divorce rate—the alarming increase in sexual sin—infidelity—yes, even adultery. We live in a day of slick, quiet, and clever sins. It is made easy to cover-up.

I recalled the solidarity of the homes of long past— when family prayer—daily devotion—the reading of the scriptures and the singing of hymns was a common practice in American homes. A practice which, I am sorry to say, has all but disappeared today.

I became saddened as I reviewed evidence of a lessening moral stability, honor, integrity, love of country—a seeking for the honors of men, of something for nothing—the tendency to lean more and more on government, the result of our ever-increasing demands, even though often economically, socially, and spiritually unsound.

There has been a nation-wide erosion of individual character. Jefferson's words still ring true:

"Material abundance without character is the surest way to destruction."

I recalled how proudly in generations past, we spoke of the "American way of life."

Then, I saw thirty million door knob hangers distributed by the Boy Scouts setting forth our political and economic rights in an effort to stimulate patriotism in this choice land. As I read this message from Freedom Foundation and the Boy Scouts of America, I thought of our basic American concepts, our constitutional government, based on a fundamental belief in God.

I became alarmed as I reviewed what has happened in our schools under so-called "Progressive Education." What about the loss of patriotism, faith in God, and the teachings of character-building principles once so much a part of our education? We have all but "forced Americanism out of the classroom to make way for temporary trivialities." (DeLove.)

I remembered President Joseph F. Smith's warning of the three dangers to the Church from within, viz., the flattery of prominent men, sexual impurity, and false educational ideas. (*Gospel Doctrine*, p. 312.)

Then there came to me the words of that courageous American patriot J. Edgar Hoover:

"Today as never before, America has need for men and women who possess the moral strength and courage of our forefathers—modern-day patriots, with pride in our country and faith in freedom. . . ."

Too often in recent years, patriotic symbols have been shunted aside. Our national heroes have been maligned, our history distorted. Has it become a disgrace to pledge allegiance to our flag—or sign a loyalty oath, or pay tribute to our national anthem? Is it shameful to encourage our children to memorize the stirring words of the men of '76? Is it becoming opprobrious to state "In God we Trust" when proclaiming our love of country?

What we desperately need today is patriotism founded on a real understanding of the American ideal—a dedicated belief in our principles of freedom, and a determination to perpetuate America's heritage.

Are we slipping from our moorings—becoming soft—carelessly drawing away from the course which has brought us such priceless blessings in days past?

David Lawrence, Editor of the *U.S. News & World Report* has said:

"The destiny of the world is in the hands of those statesmen who can interpret faithfully the commands of the Almighty."

Can our national leaders do this? Can they interpret faithfully the commands of the Almighty? Can we as citizens of this blessed land? Can we as people of the free world? Do we believe that "righteousness exalteth a nation"; that there is safety only in righteous living?

Fortunately, today we are not left in darkness. We have a guide—not only the Holy Bible, but added modern scriptures. And of the utmost importance for us today, we have the counsel and direction of living oracles. This counsel, this direction—in fact the message of the fulness of the restored gospel is being carried to the world by 12,000 ambassadors of the Lord Jesus Christ.

And what is this message? It is a world message, of the utmost importance. It is that God has again spoken from the heavens. The priesthood and authority to act in his name has been restored again to men on the earth, following centuries of darkness. The fulness of the everlasting gospel is here with all of its saving principles. To these facts I bear humble witness.

The prophets of a new gospel dispensation have counsel for us today—counsel on matters which concerned the founding fathers—freedom, liberty, righteousness which "exalteth a nation."

Do we believe and accept their counsel, or have we drifted away from those basic concepts and principles, without adherence to which, no nation can be exalted?

Elder Albert E. Bowen, said:

"That which is right does not become wrong merely because it may be deserted by the majority, neither does that which is wrong today become right tomorrow by the chance circumstance that it has won the approval or been adopted by overwhelmingly predominant numbers. Principles cannot be changed by, nor accommodate themselves to, the vagaries of popular sentiment." (*Conf. Rep.* 4-41:85.)

As a fitting conclusion to my review I sought the words of modern-day prophets. They have said much by way of counsel and warning for our guidance today.

I turned to one who has been called "a seer in the area of government" and who has stood closest to the prophet of the Lord—the President of the Church—longer than any other man in Church history. I speak of President J. Reuben Clark and I quote:

"There always comes a time when unpleasant truths must be retold, even though the retelling disturbs the ease and quiet of a luxurious error. Today seems to be such a time. On such occasions, the criticism, slander, misrepresentation that one gets, are of no consequence." (*Some Elements of Postwar American Life*.)

"Today government has touched our lives so intimately in all their relationships and all these governmental touchings have been so tabbed as political that we cannot discuss anything relating to our material welfare and existence without laying ourselves liable to the charge that we are talking politics." (*Church Section, Deseret News*, June 16, 1945.)

"I have been preaching against Communism for twenty years," said President Clark, over twenty years ago. "I still warn you against it, and I tell you that we are drifting toward it more rapidly than some of us understand, and I tell you that when Communism comes, the ownership of the things which are necessary to feed your families is going to be taken away from us. I tell you freedom of speech will go, freedom of the press will go, and freedom of religion will go.

"I have warned you against propaganda and hate. We are in the midst of the greatest exhibition of propaganda that the world has ever seen, and all directed toward one end. Just do not believe all you read." (*Conf. Rep.*, Oct. 3, 1941 and Ward Teaching Message, July 1961.)

"The plain and simple issue now facing us in America is freedom or slavery. . . . Our real enemies," said President Clark, "are *communism* and its running mate, *socialism*. And never forget for one moment that communism and socialism are state slavery. . . . One thing seems sure, we will not get out of our present difficulties without trouble, serious trouble. Indeed, it may well be that our government and its free institutions will not be preserved except at the price of life and blood. . . .

"This country faces ahead enough trouble to bring us to our knees in humble honest prayer to God for the help which he alone can give, to save us. . . . Do not think that all these usurpations, intimidations, and impositions are being done to us through inadvertency or mistake; the whole course is deliberately planned and carried out; its purpose is to destroy the Constitution and our Constitutional government. We have largely lost the conflict so far waged. But there is time to win the final victory, if we can sense our danger, and fight." (*Church Section, Deseret News,* September 25, 1949.)

Thus spoke the ever forthright and courageous, J. Reuben Clark.

And finally, and most important of all, I turned in my review to the counsel of our beloved leader—who has been an inspiration to me since boyhood—President David O. McKay—God's mouthpiece on the earth today.

"During the first half of the twentieth century," said President McKay, "we have traveled far into the soul-destroying land of socialism and made strange alliances through which we have become involved in almost continuous hot and cold wars over the whole of the earth. In this retreat from freedom the voices of protesting citizens have been drowned by raucous shouts of intolerance and abuse from those who led the retreat, and their millions of gullible youth, who are marching merrily to their doom, carrying banners on which are emblazoned such intriguing and misapplied labels as social justice, equality, reform, patriotism, social welfare." (*Church Section, Deseret News,* Oct. 18, 1952.)

"The fostering of full economic freedom lies at the base of our liberties. Only in perpetuating economic freedom can our social, political and religious liberties be preserved. . . . We must not let *complacency blind* our eyes to the real dangers threatening to destroy us." (*Ibid.,* March 2, 1952.)

"Communism is antagonistic to the American way of life. Its avowed purpose is to destroy belief in God and free enterprise," declared President McKay. "In education for citizenship, therefore, why should we not see to it that every child in America is taught the superiority of our way of life, of our Constitution and the sacredness of the freedom of the individual. Such definite instruction is not in violation of either the federal or the state constitution.

"I love the Stars and Stripes, and the American way of life. I have faith in the Constitution of the United States. I believe that only through a truly educated citizenry can the ideals that inspired the Founding Fathers of our Nation be preserved and perpetuated."

Then President McKay listed as one of the four fundamental elements in such an education "the open and forceful teaching of facts regarding communism as an enemy to God and to individual freedom." (*Ibid.*, March 13, 1954.)

President McKay has called communism the greatest threat to the Church today. (Press Conference, Hyde Park Chapel, London Feb. 24, 1961.)

Because the latest words of God's prophet are of extreme importance to the Latter-day Saints, let me in conclusion, quote very briefly and humbly from the counsel given by President McKay in the last three general conferences.

In October, 1961 President McKay gave a stirring opening address on our American way of life and the communist threat. He expressed grief and shock over a Supreme Court decision and stated that the enemies to our Republican form of government are becoming more blatant.

At the close of general conference last April President McKay emphasized that "men are rapidly classifying themselves into two groups: believers and nonbelievers." Then he quoted J. Edgar Hoover's warning:

"This nation is face to face with the greatest danger ever to confront it, a sinister and deadly conspiracy, which can be conquered only by an alert, informed citizenry. It is indeed appalling that some members of our society continue to deplore and criticize those who stress the communist danger. Public indifference to this threat is tantamount to national suicide. Lethargy leads only to disaster, knowledge of the enemy, alertness to the dangers, everyday patriotism, are the brick and mortar with which we can build an impregnable fortress against communism." (*Conf. Rep*. April 8, 1962, p. 125.)

In the last October conference President McKay said:

"In these days of uncertainty and unrest, liberty-loving peoples' greatest responsibility and paramount duty is to preserve and proclaim the freedom of the individual, his relationships to Deity, and the necessity of obedience to the principles of the gospel of Jesus Christ. Only thus will mankind find peace and happiness."

He finished his address by urging us "to support good and conscientious candidates, of either party, who are aware of the great dangers inherent in communism, and who are truly dedicated to the constitution, in the tradition of the Founding Fathers." (*Idem*.)

We cannot say that the prophet of the Lord has not warned us. President McKay has emphasized the dangers to our God-given freedom again and again. Will we heed his counsel? Are we in harmony? Do we appreciate his repeated warnings?

Every Latter-day Saint has spiritual obligations in four basic areas: his home, his church, his job, and his citizenship responsibility. Each of these areas should receive consistent attention although not necessarily equal time.

Are we doing our duty in these important fields? What about our citizenship responsibility—our obligation to safeguard our freedom and preserve the Constitution?

The Prophet Joseph Smith said the time would come when the Constitution would hang as it were by a thread.

Modern-day prophets for the last thirty years have been warning us that we have been rapidly moving in that direction. Fortunately, the Prophet Joseph Smith saw the part the elders of Israel would play in this crisis. Will there be some of us who won't care about saving the Constitution—others who will be blinded by the craftiness of men—and some who will knowingly be working to destroy it? He that has ears to hear and eyes to see can discern by the spirit, and through the words of God's mouthpiece, that our liberties are being taken.

The enemy is amongst and upon us. Zion must awake and arouse herself.

We, the elders of Israel, can be and should be the leaven in the loaf for freedom.

Years ago, President Brigham Young stated, "We all believe that the Lord will fight our battles; but how? Will he do it while we are unconcerned and make no effort whatever for our own safety when the enemy is upon us? . . . it would be quite as reasonable to expect remission of sins without baptism, as to expect the Lord to fight our battles without our taking every precaution to be prepared to defend ourselves. The Lord requires us to be quite as willing to fight our own battles as to have Him fight them for us. If we are not ready for the enemy when he comes upon us, we have not lived up to the requirements of Him who guides the ship of Zion, or who dictates the affairs of the Kingdom." (*Journal of Discourses* 11:131.)

May we as a people face courageously the challenging responsibility which faces us. "All that is necessary for the triumph of evil is that good men do nothing." (Edmund Burke.) We are not here to sit by complacently while our birthright of freedom is exchanged for a mess of socialist-communist pottage.

I love this great land—the Lord's latter-day base of operations. I love the free world—I live our Father's children everywhere.

God bless us in our stewardship. May we be at least as valiant for freedom and righteousness—here and now—as we were when we fought for these principles in the pre-existence.

There is no other safe way. "For righteousness exalteth a nation."

(*Tabernacle, Salt Lake City, Utah, April Conference,* 1963.)

The Threat of Communism

In the Old Testament we read: "My people are destroyed for lack of knowledge." (Hosea 4:6.)

Thus spoke Hosea, the prophet.

These words of warning are my text.

As in Old Testament days we need knowledge today. We need to know our enemies. We must assess clearly and accurately the perils that face the free world. At the same time we must assure ourselves of the knowledge which brings confidence and trust in our ability and that of our friends around the world to face the future—not in fear but with vigilance. From knowledge comes strength and from strength comes the power to preserve freedom both at home and abroad.

Our President and other dedicated men have worked tirelessly to help the free world understand better the deadly world conflict between good and evil which is constantly going on.

We are now entering a period of conferences, first at the summit in May and again in June when President Eisenhower travels to Moscow for a ten-day visit in Russia.

As the President said in his State of the Union Message last January, "We will continue in our search for peace and in our efforts to reach *actually enforceable agreements*."

We have an enormous responsibility here in the United States to help maintain peace and freedom and to push back the somber clouds of war-threats caused by international tensions.

The power of communism depends to a large extent on public ignorance. Knowledge is a dangerous thing—to totalitarian states; but knowledge is strength to a free people.

There are some fundamental facts which must never

be overlooked, lest it be said of this our land, "My people are destroyed for lack of knowledge."

We must never forget exactly what communism is. Communism is far more than an economic system. It is a total philosophy of life—atheistic and completely opposed to all that we hold dear.

We believe in an all-wise Creator. Communism teaches that everything in existence came about as a result of ceaseless motion of the forces of nature.

We believe in the dignity of man. Communism holds that human beings are but graduate beasts. Hence communism does not hesitate to destroy those who stand in its way. The Russian communists in their rise to power liquidated millions of their fellow countrymen. The Chinese communists wiped out tens of millions—perhaps as many as thirty million.

We believe in a moral code. Communism denies innate right or wrong. As W. Cleon Skousen has said in his timely book, *The Naked Communist*: The communist "has convinced himself that nothing is evil which answers the call of expediency." This is a most damnable doctrine. People who truly accept such a philosophy have neither conscience nor honor. Force, trickery, lies, broken promises are wholly justified.

We believe in religion as a mode of life resulting from our faith in God. Communism contends that all religion must be overthrown because it inhibits the spirit of world revolutions.

This atheistic, degrading, but militant philosophy is backed up with the strength and resources of a big country of 210 million people and a fast-growing economy. In addition, communism has built an empire of 700 million people more. Besides this, it has agents in all free world countries whose ultimate aim is to overthrow the existing social order and bring these countries under the red flag.

The major communist objective, make no mistake about

it, is to destroy any society that adheres to the fundamentals of spiritual, economic, and political freedom—the integrity of man.

As the leading exponent of this society, the United States is thus the primary target of Marxian-Lenin philosophy.

Internationally, communism seeks to isolate us from the rest of the free world. Here at home, communism ceaselessly pursues the disintegration of the American way of life. It strives to use education, science, literature, art, even the churches to undermine our free society.

Suppose for a moment that this country fell under communist control. What would be the fruits of this calamity? First the true seat of government would immediately be removed from Washington to Moscow. William Z. Foster, the former head of the Communist Party in the United States, said this: "When a Communist heads the government of the United States—and that day will come just as surely as the sun rises—the government will not be a Capitalistic government but a Soviet government, and behind this government will stand the Red Army to enforce the dictatorship of the proletariat."

What would this mean to you and me in our daily lives?

Could we own our own homes? Our living quarters would be assigned to us and we would pay rent to the state as ordered.

Could we own our own farms? Our farms would be collectivized and become the property of the state and we would work them under orders from the state.

Could we start a business and hire people to work for us? To do so would make us criminals.

Could we work where we pleased? We would work when, where, and how we were told—and the government would do the telling. No labor unions as we now know them would be permitted to exist. Neither would Chambers of Commerce, Farm Organizations, Rotary Clubs, the Elks, the American Legions and other organizations.

What would happen to our bank accounts? All above a small sum would be confiscated. The rest would be state-controlled for us. The state would take over our insurance.

Except for a few closely personal items we would have no property to leave to our families when we die.

We would travel around the country only with police permission.

We could not travel abroad or marry a foreigner without the specific approval of the state.

We could not even write freely to friends in other countries.

Our children would go to the schools selected for them, and only so long as the state permitted. Lenin said, "Give us a child for eight years, and it will be a Bolshevik forever."

Teachers would be free to teach only what the state authorized. William Z. Foster said, "Our teachers must write new school textbooks and rewrite history from the Marxian viewpoint."

To belong to a church would be sure to bring discrimination and penalties of many kinds against us and our families. The great majority of church buildings would become state museums or warehouses.

No real compromise is possible with evil such as this.

We dare not underestimate the communists' zeal, nor their aims, nor their power. To do so could mean our destruction.

We dare not accept communist pledges at face value.

The German situation is a dramatic example.

The Soviet Union in the 1940's sealed off its German occupation zone—breaking its promise.

The Soviet Union built up a powerful East German semi-military police force—breaking another promise.

The Soviet Union pledged German political freedom,

as well as freedom of speech and press. Here again she broke her promise.

The Soviet Union agreed to four-power rule in Berlin, then set up a separate East Berlin—breaking its promise.

I visited the Soviet Union last fall, spending much of my time with the good, honest, hard-working people of the soil. I am sure the Russian people want peace. I am confident that we can look forward to an era of peace if the governments of the world respond to the will of the people. But I saw no evidence that the communist leaders have altered their goal of world conquest—by economic if not by military means.

Even this short visit to the Soviet Union clearly revealed how uneven and unbalanced their economic progress actually is. Their success in the field of rocketry is in sharp contrast to their backwardness in general standards of living. A Soviet wisecrack of recent vintage goes like this: "Last year we got a sputnik and this year a lunik, and one of these days we even get shoes."

In agricultural efficiency and productivity the Soviet Union is still a long way behind the United States. But they do have a substantial growth potential.

By means of a great effort, including better economic incentives, Soviet agriculture has increased production by one-half or more in the past six years.

About fifty million persons work in Russian agriculture and forestry—more than forty percent of their total labor force—compared with a little over seven million persons in the United States, or less than ten percent of our labor force.

They have relatively few farm machines compared to the United States, and they use a great deal of hand labor, most of it done by women. Some sixty to seventy-five percent of their agricultural labor force consists of women.

One farm worker in the U. S. produces enough food and fiber to support about twenty-five persons—one farm worker in Russia produces enough for only five or six persons.

The typical Russian laborer has one pair of shoes and one suit of clothes. That's because it takes a month's wages to buy a pair of shoes and two months or more to buy a suit.

They are putting up a bold front as regards their ability to catch up. I saw hundreds of posters in the USSR urging farmers to surpass the United States in per capita production. I also saw numerous posters forecasting the ultimate victory of the communist system.

But we in this country are driving ahead also.

I feel sure that the Soviets will not equal nor surpass our productivity in our lifetime, if ever, under their system of agriculture. Why? Because they can never duplicate the levels of efficiency and productive ingenuity which are called forth in a free society.

But let us not underestimate them. On the contrary, let us strive harder to make our own free system of agriculture and industry even more efficient. And let us constantly keep our guard up.

What can you and I do to help meet this grave challenge from a godless, atheistic, cruelly materialistic system—to preserve our God-given free way of life?

First, let us all prize the treasures we have in this country. This is a choice land—all of America—choice above all others. Blessed by the Almighty, our forebears have made it so. It will continue to be a land of freedom and liberty as long as we are able and willing to advance in the light of sound and enduring principles of right.

Second, let us all do our part to stay free: Let us stand eternal watch against the accumulation of too much power in government. Here in our free land let us preserve a true climate in which man can grow.

Third, let us all reaffirm our patriotism, our love of country. Patriotism is more than flag-waving and brave words. It is how we respond to public issues. Let us rededicate ourselves as patriots in the truest sense.

Fourth, let us all help to build peace: True peace springs from within. Its price is righteousness, and to achieve righteousness we must so conduct ourselves individually and collectively as to earn the loyalty and devotion of other men.

Finally, let us all rededicate our lives and our nation to do the will of God. With each of you, I love this nation. It is my firm belief that the God of heaven guided the founding fathers in establishing it for his particular purposes. But God's purpose is to build people of character, not physical monuments to their material accumulations.

Nations that truly love freedom love God. History is replete with examples of once powerful nations that have forgotten God. No nation ripened in iniquity can long endure. "Righteousness exalteth a nation; but sin is a reproach to any people." (Proverbs 14:34.)

We in this land have a heritage of freedom. It has rewarded us beyond our brightest dreams. The key to further progress—the key to national security—is the preservation of the initiative, vitality, energy, and resourcefulness of our people. Our material progress is merely a by-product of our freedom. Our God-given freedom, a basic principle of religious truth, is still the most powerful force on the face of the earth.

I feel sure that the people of the world want peace—and I specifically include the people of Russia.

That is why we can approach these talks with the Russians with inner strength but without illusions. We know that knowledge of the enemy teaches us wariness and caution; we know too that we speak for millions of suppressed people on the Soviet side of the iron curtain, all those everywhere who want peace with human dignity.

Any system which deprives men of their free agency, which weakens the home and family, which depends on butchery for power, which denies all moral responsibility, which holds that man lives by bread alone, and which denies the existence of God, is of the devil.

This is the communist philosophy. There is no real evidence that it has been changed in the last forty years.

Knowledge of the enemy and of ourselves give us the strength to fight the good fight for freedom and world peace.

May it never come to pass that "My people are destroyed for lack of knowledge," I humbly pray.

(Tabernacle, Salt Lake City, Utah, April Conference, 1960.)

The Real Challenge

Samuel Johnson, the English writer, once said that "a man seldom thinks with more earnestness of anything than he does of his dinner."

While many of us might view that opinion as more witty than wise, I believe we would agree that scientists, statesmen and social observers are thinking with unusual earnestness today about dinner in the future—about the problem of food and people—or, as some prefer to put it, the problem of food, people and peace.

There's an old saying: "A hungry people listens not to reason, nor cares for justice, nor is bent by any prayers." If this be true, it perhaps follows that what the world does about food may be the very heart of its hopes for permanent peace.

For this reason, among many others, I am glad to be with you this evening to discuss this basic problem.

By way of presenting my credentials, I am forced to introduce a personal note into these remarks. So I should like to begin by telling you that during my term of office as Secretary of Agriculture, I made seven trade trips abroad, visiting more than forty countries—in Latin America, the Far East, Europe, the Middle East, countries all around the world.

I wish I could help you visualize what I saw on those trips—the refugees in Hong Kong, Calcutta, and Karachi—the hungry, the homeless, the unwanted and abandoned—the great contrast between rich and poor in Latin America and the Orient.

But my interest in the food and people problem goes back still farther. In 1946, I was one of 130 delegates from thirty-one countries who met in the first International Conference of Farm Organizations at Church House in Lon-

don. I tell you, ladies and gentlemen, in those days just
following World War II, for many of the world's people
life was a *five* letter word, and it was spelled w-h-e-a-t!

I remember Sir John Boyd Orr—later John Lord Orr and
the Director General of the Food and Agricultural Organization of the United Nations—saying: "From now on we shall
begin to lift the world out of scarcity." But at that time it
seemed there could never be enough food to meet even the
minimum requirements of the hungry.

I spent that year of 1946 in Europe, directing relief
activities for our church membership in fourteen nations.
Unless you were there, it would be impossible to appreciate
how terrible conditions were at the end of the war in much
of Europe. And I didn't see it at its worst.

But I saw plenty. I saw nations still in collapse—
cities lying in ghastly ruin—the big railway stations reduced to twisted steel and rubble—the universities, opera
houses, museums, art galleries, palaces smashed into masses
of wreckage.

But by far the worst wreckage had been wrought on the
people. You could glimpse it in the twitching faces, the
fear-haunted eyes, the ruined reflexes, the loss of spirit.
You would see a pedestrian standing in the street, squarely
in the path of an approaching automobile—just standing
there, seemingly unable to move out of the way. His legs
wouldn't obey his brain, or maybe his brain didn't care
any more whether he lived or died. The car would come
to a halt, and then slowly, pathetically, he would shuffle to
the curb.

And the children, though they came around faster
than the adults, showed on their little, old faces the horror
engendered by the wailing sirens, the earth-shaking bombs,
the dreadful pressure of constant fear and years of
malnutrition.

I remember meeting with our people in Karlsruhe,
Hamburg, Berlin, Vienna, and in the cities of Poland and

Czechoslovakia. We met in cold, bombed-out buildings, without light, without heat. I visited the living quarters of some of the refugees—and there were as many as twenty-two persons—four complete families—living in one room.

The first food we were able to get for our people was bought from the Swiss Government. I have never been able to describe to anyone what it meant to them. How do you describe what food means to a starving person! And they were *starving*, some of them—not just hungry, but close to the last stages of starvation.

I remember—because I can never forget—the arrival of our first church welfare supplies in Berlin from the United States. I took one of the men, Richard Ranglack, by the arm and we walked down to the old battered warehouse that was under the control of the International Red Cross. Armed guards stood at the corners, and it was their rifles that prevented stealing and looting—because the people of Berlin were half-crazed from hunger. As we entered the warehouse, we walked to the far end, and there we saw boxes piled almost to the ceiling.

"Are those boxes of food?" Richard asked, "Do you mean to tell me those boxes are full of food?"

"Yes," I replied, "food and clothing and bedding—and, I hope, a few medical supplies."

We took down some of the boxes, Richard and I together. We opened one, and it was filled with the commonest of common food, cracked wheat, with nothing added or taken away, just as the Lord made it and intended it to be.

As that good man saw that life-giving wheat, he couldn't help putting his hands into it, and running it through them—and suddenly he broke down and began to cry like a little child.

We opened another box, and this was filled with dried beans. And again he touched them. And then after a moment he looked me full in the face through his tearful eyes—and mine were wet, too—and he said, slowly shaking his head, "Brother Benson, it is hard to believe that people who have never seen us could do so much for us."

I tell you these things to indicate that I have seen this problem of food and people firsthand. I know what it is— how serious it is—how difficult—how necessary it is to resolve it—but I know, too, that it can't be resolved by catchwords or oversimplification or by disregarding basic economic laws.

Unfortunately, too many people are attempting to solve it in that way. That seems to have been the tendency from the time of Malthus to the present.

You recall that in 1798, Thomas Malthus, who was then a young English clergyman, published a treatise entitled "Essay on the Principle of Population as It Affects the Future Improvement of Society." Malthus thought he had made a great social discovery, namely that:

"Population increases in a geometrical or doubling or multiplying proportion, such as: 2, 4, 8, 16, 32, 64. The production of food on the other hand, increases arithmetically, or by addition: 2, 4, 6, 8, 10, 12."

Malthus concluded that—with population tending to double every generation while food production plodded along at a relatively slow rate—people would overtax the food-producing ability of the world. It would, that is, unless population growth was checked by famine, disease, war, vice, late marriages, or some other cause.

The Malthusian theory proved to be a gross oversimplification.

As time passed, it became evident that population was growing, yes, but not nearly so fast as Malthus had feared. Meantime, the development of the New World and an agricultural revolution of a sort in the Old, plus better means of distribution, provided Europe and America with more food per person than they had ever had before. Until a few decades ago, therefore, the Malthusian theory seemed definitely out the window.

In the past two or three decades, however, world population has spurted ahead so rapidly that the question has again arisen whether Malthus was right after all. So today we find a great deal of discussion and a great many questions. Will population outrun food? Will people one, two, or three generations hence be doomed to a coolie standard of living? Is mankind fighting a desperate rear guard action in a vain effort to keep just one short step ahead of the rapidly oncoming forces of famine?

Some well-known persons answer yes—and they advocate drastic steps by government action to limit population growth. They contend that the world must stabilize its population or many must starve. In short, the only course that can save mankind from disaster lurking just around the corner is the worldwide adoption by government of population restriction policies.

This, I firmly believe, is again unrealistic and dangerous oversimplification. It is inconceivable to me that the problem of food and people either will, or can, be solved in this way. For one thing, the right to marry and have a family, and to determine the size of one's family in accordance with one's conscience and legitimate desires is so fundamental that I just can't visualize people permitting government to tamper with it. The whole thing smacks of government interference at its totalitarian worst. I agree wholeheartedly with President Eisenhower's position that it is not the business of the United States Government to enter this area.

Moreover, the available facts do not support the notion that mankind must become increasingly sterile or starve. Those who are fond of projecting population trends into the future never seem willing to do the same for food production trends. They concentrate their gaze on the *people* side of the equation and blind themselves to the *food* side. It is true that there has been a population explosion of sorts in recent decades. But there has been an even greater *agricultural technological explosion*—not only in the United States but also in the world in general. The population explosion is running substantially behind the agricultural explosion—and the agricultural explosion is just beginning.

Now, don't misunderstand this as meaning that the problem of people and food can be dismissed out of hand as simply a question of better distribution of food. Some nations have surpluses, others have deficits—bring them together, and the problem disappears. This, too, is an unrealistic and dangerous oversimplification. The problem neither will, nor can be, solved by taking our agricultural surpluses and those of Canada, Australia, Argentina, and other food and fiber-exporting countries and shipping them overseas to the needy.

For one thing, there just isn't that much surplus currently available—though there is certainly that much productive capacity available. For another, there are limitations on how much the needy areas can absorb, because of their insufficient port facilities, inadequate warehousing, lack of refrigeration, poor transportation from ports to inland regions, and cultural resistance to changing their food habits. Many of the world's malnourished people, for example, just don't know how to use wheat. Then there are difficulties as to who is to pay the bills and how to prevent the disruption of normal markets.

Of extreme importance in reaching a solution are our own US Agricultural policies. We are the undoubted world leader in agriculture. How we exercise our leadership will have tremendous effect on the food and people problem. We must keep our agriculture *free—dynamic—expanding—growing in efficiency and productivity*. We cannot do this by strapping it more and more firmly into the straitjacket of government controls. How sad it is to see forces in our government trying to move toward more controls, more centralization, more government interference and dictation in agriculture when the folly of that course is clearly indicated by the failures of controlled agriculture in Russia, China, Cuba, Hungary, and other nations.

The area to concentrate on is the building of markets and the wise use of our agricultural abundance and the generous sharing of our agricultural know-how. These are of inestimable importance now and in the years just ahead. It was because we recognized this fact that we began under President Eisenhower the Food for Peace Program.

I believe that history will record Food for Peace as a milestone, a turning point, the beginning of a sound, aggressive, and realistic effort to come to grips with the problem of food and people.

Food for Peace is not so much a new progrm as a new emphasis. The food relief operations administered by Herbert Hoover after World War I were, in a sense, a food for peace program. The post World War II food relief program was also a food for peace operation. Both these operations were geared to emergency situations of world need.

With the Agricultural Trade Development and Assistance Act of 1954—commonly known as Public Law 480— we entered a new phase. The world emergency was past. There was no longer immediate danger of widespread starvation. But there was still an urgency for better nutrition. P.L. 480 envisioned maximum sales through competitive markets and gave us authority not only to donate food and fiber to the needy and to barter it for other commodities, but also to sell vast amounts of surplus food and fiber either for foreign currency or on credit. Many countries didn't have dollars to buy our farm products. This new program enabled them to buy with their own currency. Within three years after its adoption, US shipments of farm products abroad went up 70 percent.

The Food for Peace Program—which began in 1959—

continued, intensified, and gave new direction to these activities.

One of my proudest moments as Secretary of Agriculture came when we got President Eisenhower's OK on this program.

We had been pushing it for many months in Cabinet and elsewhere against the opposition of some who feared it might become a food-dumping program. Not until the day before President Eisenhower's 1959 message on agriculture went to the Congress was the issue resolved.

At the last minute, the President added to his message a paragraph which said in part, "Food can be a powerful instrument for all the world in building a durable peace. . . . I am setting steps in motion to explore anew with other surplus-producing nations all practical means of utilizing the various agricultural surpluses of each in the interest of reinforcing peace and the well-being of friendly peoples throughout the world—in short, using food for peace."

Thus was born one of the most far-reaching and popular concepts of the Eisenhower administration.

Food for Peace is the whole complex of activities under which we, by ourselves, or in co-operation with other nations, are endeavoring to lift world nutritional levels. The most spectacular achievement of the program thus far has been the four year wheat-rice agreement negotiated by the United States and India in May, 1960. It is by far the biggest grain deal in history—amounting to 1 billion 300 million dollars. Under it, we agreed to ship India—for their currency—587 million bushels of wheat—that's half a US wheat crop—and 22 million hundredweight of rice—that's half a US rice crop.

It means that on the average a shipload of food a day— for four years—is moving to India under this one deal.

In the donation area, during 1960, twenty private agencies such as CARE, various religious agencies, and others distributed dry milk, flour, cornmeal, rice, and other foods donated by the government to more than 60 million persons in over ninety countries. No nation under heaven has ever been so generous with its abundance.

In the area of international co-operation, Argentina, Australia, Canada, France, and the United States organized a Wheat Utilization Committee. Its purpose was to promote the more effective use of wheat in improving diets and fostering the economic development of newly emerging countries.

Another phase of Food for Peace—and in the long run the most important phase—involves helping needy nations produce more of their own food supplies. More than 1,000 United States agricultural technicians are working in many of these lands bringing American farming know-how to their farmers. And large amounts of the foreign currencies obtained through P.L. 480 sales are being lent back or granted to foreign governments for economic development including agricultural improvement.

I am very proud of what has been, and is being, done under Food for Peace. Market development programs of the various commodity groups in co-operation with government have been effective in expanding our markets. Do you know, for example, that the school lunch idea has spread from the United States to Japan? In Tokyo I saw a thousand children eating a school lunch, mostly of bread and milk produced on American farms.

I saw mobile kitchens in Japan, kitchens mounted in buses. They were equipped with loud speakers, and the Japanese women came around with their children strapped to their backs, to learn how to prepare bargain United States farm product dishes. United States wheat, soy beans, and dairy products have now become important foods in Japan.

Our food—whether bought for dollars or foreign currency or on credit, and whether bartered or donated—is a tremendous ambassador of goodwill. It was, and is, helping the free world stay free. It was, and is, helping feed the hungry and clothe the naked. It was, and is, helping newly developing nations to get on their feet.

I am happy to see Food for Peace being continued and, as we recommended, expanded by the Kennedy Administration. I only wish other phases of the Kennedy farm proposals were equally sound.

Why do we regard Food for Peace as such an immensely hopeful step toward the eventual solution of the food and people problem—worldwide? It is partly because of what the program is doing and partly because of what it implies.

That this program is possible derives from the fact that now, for the first time in mankind's long history, a large segment of the world's people have at last escaped permanently from the fear of hunger and malnutrition caused by general shortages of food. This is an earth-shaking achievement that became a promise during the past twenty years and an actual achievement during the past ten. For one-third of the world's people—those living in the thirty industrialized countries of the temperate northern area of the earth—agricultural production and production of goods they can trade for food permanently assures their food supply.

If their resources are not destroyed by war, these nations now have the science, the technology, the facilities, the services, the industrial and agricultural plant, the financial resources, and the management know-how to feed themselves regardless of their population growth.

These are the conclusions reached by technicians and scientists of the USDA after a world-wide survey of food needs and productive capacity.

Actually, food supplies for the United States, Canada, Australia, New Zealand, and northwestern Europe have been reasonably adequate for considerably longer than the past two decades. But only in the past ten to twenty years has this same security been achieved for Eastern Europe and Japan. In the seven years ending in 1961, Japan increased its agricultural production *per capita* by an average of five percent *a year*—and Eastern Europe by 2.7 percent a year.

Agriculture in the industrialized nations has experienced a technological revolution of almost fantastic proportions when compared with the past. And all indications are that it is still in its beginnings.

There is every reason to believe, moreover, that this agricultural achievement can now be extended—with modern means of communication extended rapidly—to the remaining peoples of the earth. I venture to say that if the governments of the world were to devote a sizeable fraction of the research, funds, and efforts to the problem of cracking the world food problem that they now devote to nuclear experiments, explorations in space, and landing on the moon, the problem might even be well-nigh solved before the end of the present decade.

Even without such a crash program, there is every reason to expect that long before the close of the present century there will be adequate food supplies for all the peoples of the earth, regardless of the population increase. It is no longer a question of physical resources or know-how. It is basically a question of determination to get the job done. It reminds me of President Eisenhower's oft-quoted remark, "It's not the size of the dog in the fight that's important. It's the size of the fight in the dog."

The food problems of the deficit nations arise out of a low stage of agricultural and industrial development—and this in turn from depleted soils, lack of fertilizers and other agricultural materials, poor communication, and inadequate educational and health facilities resulting in illiteracy and low physical energy.

All of these deficiencies can be remedied—and at the pace with which the modern world moves, remedied relatively quickly. Poor, depleted, and eroded land can swiftly be made productive. I have seen United States farmers take poor land that was producing 30 to 35 bushels of corn

an acre and *in one year*—by intensive fertilization and other
cultural practices—raise the yield to 125 bushels or more.

The Department of Agriculture estimates that the
people of the deficit areas of the world who—in addition to
a shortage of animal products and vegetable oils—now have
an annual shortage of other food crops equivalent to 29 million tons of wheat, could produce this quantity of wheat on
the arable land presently available to them by the use of
roughly 2 million tons of nitrogen and one million tons of
phosphoric acid. To build within these countries fertilizer
plants adequate to provide these requirements at present
costs of construction, would, it is estimated, require an
expenditure of about $1.65 billion. In terms of modern
expenditures for armament, for defense, and for space ex-
ploration this is indeed a small sum.

Up to ten years ago, the farmers of India used almost
no fertilizer at all. Now they are demanding it. Though
India still uses only one-fiftieth as much fertilizer an acre
as Western Europe, during the past ten years production
of food in India has increased 60 percent. Yet the productivity
of the average Indian farm in terms of yields an acre and
per head of livestock is still among the lowest in the world.
The average milk production per cow in India is only about
750 pounds a year. In the US, it is ten times that high.

The underdeveloped nations have long neglected agriculture. We in the United States have roughly 100,000
employees—more than would be needed under a free agriculture—in the U.S.D.A.—devoted to aiding agriculture.
Until just recently India had one government agricultural
officer per state district—and some of these districts are as
large as Belgium or Holland.

To sum it up, an immensely more productive agriculture throughout these areas awaits only effective programs
to bring about more and better use of water, more effective
drainage, more fertilizer and insecticides, better seeds, and
equipment, and an efficient program of education in agri-

cultural techniques much as is provided by our own extension service.

Because of all these developments, I do not believe there is cause for pessimism about the world's ability to feed itself better and better as time goes on. First, the agricultural revolution, even in the most advanced nations, is only just getting well under way. In much of the world, it has hardly started. Second, even in the United States, science has never really been turned loose on agriculture as it has on industry. The total of public and private funds spent on food and agriculture research this fiscal year is estimated at about $600 million. This is the *total*. It includes Federal and State research—plus all private research. It is $168 million less than the Federal Government paid farmers last year to cut down their acres of corn and grain sorghums. It is less than one-fifth of the United States Government's 1961 expenditures for price support.

We have hardly scratched, not the surface, but the thinnest skin of the very top layer of the surface, compared with what could conceivably be done to enhance food supplies. We have in the United States 458 million acres classed as cropland. Last year, we grew crops on only about 295 million of those acres—the smallest use of our cropland since the records began.

In terms of numbers, we have fewer persons working in agriculture than at any time since the Civil War.

In the near future we shall probably be using sea water for irrigation and other uses—and in the not too distant future we will, if desirable, be able to farm the oceans.

I believe that the answer to hunger is food. A decade, a generation, a century hence, the capacity to produce per capita abundance can, I believe, dwarf our most hopeful imaginings.

But much will depend on our own economic and agricultural policies.

What I view as a desperately serious threat to our,

and the world's future well-being is the erosion of our free economic system, specifically of our free agriculture.

Next to war, which destroys resources, the greatest threat to the world's coming abundance would be the loss of freedom, both political and economic. Such a loss would fasten a ball and chain on initiative and efficiency, restricting the present use of resources and hampering their further development. This, for us, is the real challenge.

For eight years, between 1953 and 1961, we strove to maintain and enhance the freedom of American agriculture. During those eight years, the nation witnessed the biggest expansion of farm markets ever achieved in any comparable period. The nation also witnessed the greatest increase in agricultural productivity per man-hour. When we took office, one farmer, on the average, was providing food and fiber for 17 persons. When we left office, one farmer, on the average, was providing food and fiber for 26 persons.

And during those eight years, the world saw its greatest development in the use of Food for Peace.

United States agriculture is a giant when it is free, but government policy today aims to envelop it in bigger and bigger fetters, controls, and chains. And the spirit in which the choice is presented is one of: Take these controls or we'll break you. The Congress last year refused to go along with recommendations that would have made the Secretary of Agriculture a virtual dictator over United States farmers. This year, the proposals are for strong controls over feed grains, wheat and dairy production, and the original proposal even contained a provision for jail sentences.

I do not mean to say that the Federal Government should be an aloof spectator so far as agriculture is concerned. I do say it must not become a dictator. It must not smother or usurp the functions of individual or co-operative effort, initiative, and leadership.

Most of the government programs affecting agriculture

fall into two broad groups. In one group are programs designed to increase farmers' ability to serve, such as research, education, conservation, electrification.

They benefit not only farmers but also the people in general. They produce a better product—find new uses for crops—enable farmers to grow more units per acre, more meat per animal, more milk per cow, more eggs per hen. They result in food and fiber of better quality—food that is more nutritious—fiber that is better fitted to specific uses.

They expand existing markets—create new markets. They cut marketing costs—reduce spoilage in transportation, handling, and processing.

Programs that produce such results improve the diets of the world's people. The progress we have made in agriculture has come about through programs of this type.

Programs of the second type are intended primarily to improve here and now the relative prices and incomes received by farmers—usually by controls over production. Realistic price supports and limited voluntary controls can be useful in promoting orderly marketing and fostering stability of farm income. But they can also be misused—by relying upon them as cure-alls—by overemphasizing them as is being done today. In this case they cause more problems than they solve. They involve the government in the production, marketing, and price making of farm products. They increase costs. They decrease efficiency. They steadily encroach on farmers' freedom.

If the voices of 15 million farm people in America could be crystallized into one voice, it would, I feel sure, demand more freedom.

That voice would say:

Give us more freedom to plant—so that we can run our farms efficiently and improve national and world diets.

Give us more freedom to market—so that we can increase our incomes.

Give us more freedom to meet our competition—so that we can expand our markets.

Give us more freedom from government interference—so that we may again be independent and self-reliant.

That is the voice of faith—the farmer's *faith* in his own ability to meet changing economic conditions with a minimum of government help—the farmer's *faith* in the future of agriculture and of America—the same basic faith that energized the American people from the beginning of this nation.

I say to you that our agriculture will never reach its full strength—and full capacity to serve mankind—until farmers have the essential freedom to plant, to market, to compete, and to make their own decisions.

Farmers want to produce for markets, not for government bounty.

Farmers want government at their sides, not on their backs.

Farmers know that the farms of America cannot be run from a desk in Washington.

Farmers know better than any other group that socialized regimentation strikes with deadly aim at the very heart of our free agriculture and the free enterprise principles which are basic to the high American standard of living and the future we seek.

Farmers know that controls breed more controls. Along with the controls comes the inevitable corps of bureaucratic inspectors. Farmers don't want milk allotments and cow quotas. They don't want the deadening hand of Big Government clamping down ever more heavily upon their precious freedom.

This, I repeat, is for us in the year 1962, the real challenge.

The same basic principle applies to the world.

The world's people are awakening to the hope that

their long-awaited basic wants and needs *can* be satisfied—and their wants range far beyond food, shelter, and clothing.

An ancient of the Far East put it this way: "We want rice and respect—but we want respect first."

The greatest material contribution the industrialized nation can make to world peace and world progress is to join hands in helping the underdeveloped nations of the world help themselves. This cannot be done by giving away food surpluses indiscriminately—by destroying free competitive markets. It cannot be done by putting these nations on a food relief dole, which undermines their self-respect.

We and the other industrialized nations have a tremendous opportunity to use our abundance as capital to help the newly emerging nations develop their own agriculture and industry.

We can use food to help them build dams for electric power and irrigation, roads for better transportation and communication, plants for the production of fertilizer, weed killers, insecticides, and farm machinery.

This is what we are striving to do in the Food for Peace program.

My hope, my belief, and my fervent prayer are that we will succeed.

In closing, I give you these words of the President under whom I served for eight busy, fruitful years.

"The peace we seek, founded upon decent trust and co-operative effort among nations, can be fortified, not by weapons of war but by wheat and by cotton, by milk and by wool, by meat and by timber and by rice. . . ."

God speed us on our way toward this worthy objective.

(*Buffalo Council on World Affairs, Buffalo, New York,* May 15, 1962.)

World Brotherhood

This opportunity to meet with you of the Rotary and Kiwanis Clubs and the Salt Lake City Chamber of Commerce is both a privilege and a challenging responsibility.

Your great organizations are built on the idea of service and good fellowship—and service and good fellowship, of course, are ultimately based on the noble ideal of human brotherhood. It is largely about brotherhood that I would speak with you today. This is a subject which I am sure is very close to your hearts, as it is also close to mine.

Perhaps never in history has the need for co-operation, understanding, and goodwill among all people—nations and individuals alike—been so urgent as today.

It is not only fitting—it is imperative—that we emphasize the ideal of brotherhood, and the reality of brotherhood, and the responsibility that the fact of human brotherhood confers upon us all.

The trouble with our world today is that too many people—and too many nations—either reject the idea of human brotherhood, or regard it not as a fact, but as a pretty theory. That is why the future is troubled and peace is so elusive.

Abraham Lincoln once said, "All good intelligent people are very much alike.

"Why," he asked, "should there not be patient confidence in the ultimate justice of the people; is there any better or equal hope in the world?" I feel sure that the basis of his confidence in the people was his awareness of the central fact that all men are indeed brothers.

In holy writ we read that God "hath made of one blood all nations of men for to dwell on all the face of the earth." (Acts 17:26.) God being the Father of our spirits, makes us brothers.

Over the past fourteen years I have visited a great many countries of the world—in Europe—in Latin America—and in Asia. In 1946, on a mission for the Church, I traveled and stayed in thirteen European countries for almost a year. In 1955, I visited nine nations in Latin America. In the fall of 1957, with members of my family and staff, I made a trade development trip to twelve countries, including India and Japan—a trip which took me completely around the world. And last year on another trade development trip, I visited seven European countries, including the communist nations of Russia, Yugoslavia, and Poland.

In these travels to many countries I have found what Lincoln said to be true: People are very much alike. Whether in the United States or Canada, Venezuela or Costa Rica, Japan or India, Germany or Finland, Poland or Russia—people are fundamentally the same.

They long for peace.

They love their families.

They want to live better.

They have a basic impulse to do good.

They have, in short, a fundamental appreciation of human brotherhood.

Indeed, as Carlyle wrote, "A mystic band of brotherhood makes all men one."

In all these countries, and in particular among the so-called common people, I found a warm spirit of friendliness and a high regard for the United States.

I say to you that brotherhood is a fact.

I was deeply touched by the sincerity of the welcome given us by the farmers and working people of the three communist countries we visited last fall—Yugoslavia, Poland, and the Soviet Union. A sturdy old Yugoslav farmer stood in his little home, crowded with his neighbors and representatives of the American press, and with deep emotion asked Mrs. Benson and me to convey his wishes of goodwill to you here in the United States—he was testifying to brotherhood.

A farmer in Poland insisted on sending from his meager crops a gift of fruit and nuts to America—he, too, was testifying.

We often say, and it is true, that it is not the gift but the spirit of the giver that counts. The spirit of that farmer in Yugoslavia and that farmer in Poland made their goodwill offering very touching indeed.

I think I will never forget, as long as I live, an incident in a church in Moscow on the last night of our stay in that city. With tear-stained faces, yet in voices filled with fervent hope, some 1500 Russian Christians sang a favorite hymn of my childhood: "God Be with You, till We Meet Again." They testified to the fact of brotherhood most dramatically of all. I will tell you more about this inspiring incident later.

Everywhere we went we encountered a lively curiosity, on the part of the youngsters as well as the adults. People want to know more about other people. They want to understand us, even as we want to understand them. There is, I believe, a deep-seated intuition that peace and mutual understanding go hand in hand. Meetings between representatives of different countries, whether of the highest rank as in the case of President Eisenhower and Chairman Khrushchev, or of lower official and unofficial status, stir up in the people deep-seated and sincere longings for enduring peace.

We are contributing strongly to the cause of peace by sharing our abundance with other nations. Since 1953 we have moved out of surplus an astounding $17.5 billion worth of farm commodities.

Under various government programs we have exported over $7 billion worth of farm products. This is in addition to our export sales for dollars.

We have donated to the needy abroad nearly $2 billion worth of farm products.

In the past fiscal year some sixty million people in ninety-one foreign countries received such donations. They were distributed by United States voluntary agencies in the name of the people of the United States.

This is a tremendous ambassador of goodwill. It is a concrete affirmation of our belief as a nation in the brotherhood of man. This is truly using Food for Peace.

No nation under heaven has ever been so generous to other nations with its abundance. I am proud of it, and I think every American who knows the story is proud of it, too.

The surpluses came into our hands largely because of unsound farm programs which we inherited and which tied our hands during a large part of the past seven years. Our hands are still tied by unsound wheat legislation despite our repeated recommendations for long-needed changes. But we have been able to move a tremendous quantity of surplus commodities out of government warehouses and into use because the purpose of production is consumption. A government warehouse is not a market. And at the same time we have been ironing out the defects in the farm programs and endeavoring to bring about a better balance between production and market demand.

Trade between nations is a very important agency for peace. Not only does it raise world standards of living—it also makes for deeper mutual understanding. That is why I have gone on world trade and market development trips to some thirty countries. And that is why I am going to do more of this in coming months. Such personal visits—personal contacts—are vitally important. This was thoroughly impressed upon us in the course of our trip last fall.

In the Soviet Union, for example, we were given a most warm and hospitable welcome by agricultural officials and farm people alike. The people were friendly, enthusiastic, and genuinely interested in us. I was truly impressed by the repeated emphasis in Russia upon the urgency of peace.

I cannot help believing that it was genuine and sincere on the part of the people. We can, indeed we must, build on this foundation.

In a speech in Moscow I emphasized that "People who live on the soil are much the same everywhere. In all countries they wish one thing above all—the right to live in peace and do their work. This is true in the United States. I am sure it is equally true in Russia."

I said to Mr. Khrushchev and Mr. Matskevich when they visited the United States, "I look forward to seeing your farms and to grasping in friendship and brotherhood the hands of the men and women who till them. All men should be brothers. I think no brotherhood is stronger than that of the people who cultivate the soil."

This theme I repeated over and over on the trip, and I feel sure that it was warmly received by the farmers of Russia.

As I reported to President Eisenhower and the Cabinet on my return: If the leaders of the world follow the will of the people, they will work for peace.

This does not mean that the United States, or the free world, can afford to be complacent. We saw no evidence that the communist leaders have altered their goal of world conquest, by economic if not by military means. Eternal vigilance remains the price of freedom today and always. We must keep our guard up.

But we did see, and I cannot repeat it too often, evidence of what Lincoln called "the ultimate justice of the people"— a longing for a stronger brotherhood.

In Poland, for example, we saw tragedy and hope existing side by side. It is truly pathetic that a people, who have so yearned for freedom as the Poles have done, must now live under a regime where the socialization of farming, as well as industry, is the announced goal. But it is hopeful to find the Polish peasantry sincerely devoted to private ownership of the land. These friendly peasants opened their small homes to us, gave us flowers picked from their gardens, and, as I mentioned earlier, shared with us fruits from their orchards.

One farm woman, on a load of potatoes—their diet is largely of cereals and potatoes—I remember well, said it was good that American officials should show interest in "simple folks like us." She and her husband were typical of Poland's farmers. They staunchly support private ownership of the land. They operate about twenty-five acres, using horses for motive power. There are only about 60,000 tractors in all of Poland, and of these only a few thousand are privately owned. Though the government is endeavoring to organize the small farms around machinery and marketing co-operatives called "Farmers' Circles," the peasants are wary of joining. They remember the efforts at collectivization of the post-war period.

Even in the Soviet Union, despite the large state and co-operative farms, it was very obvious that the peasants still have a deep, well-nigh indestructible desire to own and till their own soil. No doubt this is related to the fact that family ties have always been strong among the Russians, especially in the Ukraine.

But despite their longing for freedom, the Russian people are responding to their government's urgings to overtake and outstrip us in agricultural and industrial production.

We saw hundreds of posters in the USSR urging farmers to surpass the United States in per capita production. We also saw numerous posters forecasting the ultimate victory of the communist system.

Having seen agriculture under contrasting forms of government in three communist countries, I am all the more convinced of the superiority of our system of privately owned family farms, the profit motive, competitive markets, and freedom for the farmer to decide what he wants to grow and market.

The Soviets will not equal or surpass our productivity in our lifetime, if ever, under their system of agriculture. Why? Because they can never duplicate the levels of efficiency and productive ingenuity which are called forth in a free society. But we must be very sure that we preserve our own precious freedom.

Do we dare take it for granted that our freedom will be preserved? Are we so sure of it that we can pay little or no heed to the forces constantly whittling down our freedom? In our concentration upon material acquisitions, are we forgetting the spiritual bases upon which our prosperity and security rest?

All that we hold dearest in our way of life is based on spiritual truth. Our heritage of liberty is not man-made. It is God-given. Free agency is an eternal principle. Next to life itself, I am most grateful for this gift of free agency. It is more to be prized than any other earthly possession.

The advances this country has made have been the fruit of liberty—our free enterprise system—our American way of life—our God-given freedom of choice. The progress of the future must stem from this same basic blessing.

But to be enjoyed, freedom must be continually won. The major responsibility of government is to guard the lives and safeguard the freedom of its citizens. Yet even in the operation of government—especially big government—there are real dangers to our liberty.

Today the scope and variety of governmental operations have become amazingly wide. We are touched by government from before we are born until after we die. Government impinges on our lives every hour of the day and night.

Most of these governmental activities are helpful in greater or lesser degree. But we must be aware of the price we pay when we place more and more of our lives in the hands of centralized government.

We have seen in the past quarter century a tremendous shift from individual to governmental responsibility in many phases of economic and social life. We have seen a rapid shift of responsibility from the States to the Federal Government.

Deep in their hearts, the American people instinctively know that great concentration of power is an evil and a dangerous thing. They do not need to have it proved.

What lies behind this conviction? Basically, it is an intuitive knowledge that, sooner or later, the accumulation of power in a central government leads to a loss of freedom. Once power is concentrated, even for helpful purposes, it is all there, in one package, where it can be grabbed by those who may not be helpful in its use.

Our abundant material blessings have come to us through an economic system which rests largely on three pillars:

1. Free enterprise—the right to venture—to choose.
2. Private property—the right to own.
3. A market economy—the right to exchange.

Our economic order is not perfect, because it is operated by imperfect human beings. But it has given our people more of the good things of life than any other system. We must never make the catastrophic blunder of putting the chains of big government on our basic economic freedom. Yet there is that very danger today.

The pillars of our economic system are being threatened by a strange and unlikely coalition of subversives, do-gooders, and self-servers.

There are, in this country, a hard core of subversives who hate the free enterprise system and are dedicated to its overthrow. There is a host of do-gooders, who constantly criticize our free choice system, ready to solve all human problems with legislation, willing to impose their version of the millennium on you and me, unwilling to rely on the judgment of the individual. There are the self-servers, who view government as a way to gain an advantage, to restrain competition, or to obtain special favors.

But the most dangerous threat of all comes from the disinterested, that great group of otherwise intelligent people who shrug off any responsibility for public affairs.

Edmund Burke once said:

"All that is necessary for the forces of evil to win in the world is for enough good men to do nothing."

I wish all other groups in the country were as alert to the threat against freedom as are our farmers. If the voices of twenty-one million farm people in the United States could be united in one voice, that voice I feel certain would say:

Give us more freedom to plant—so that we can run our farms efficiently.

Give us more freedom to market—so that we can increase our incomes.

Give us more freedom to meet our competition—so that we can expand our markets.

Give us more freedom from government interference—so that we may be independent and self-reliant.

The history of all mankind shows very clearly that if we would be free—and if we would stay free—we must stand eternal watch against the accumulation of too much power in government. A completely planned and subsidized economy is the surest way to weaken initiative, discourage industry, destroy character, and demoralize a people. The real test of any policy is how will it affect the morale and character of the people.

I have seen in many parts of the world people who have lost their freedom. It is heart-rending. I will never forget it. I pray God it will never happen here.

Let me close by telling you about the incident in the Moscow church to which I referred earlier. On our last evening in Moscow we visited one of the two Baptist churches in the city. This church, located on a dark side street, was filled. People were standing in the hall, in the entry, even in the street. After our party was seated, the minister invited me to address the congregation.

I don't remember all that I said, but I extended greetings from the millions and millions of church people in America and around the world. I affirmed my own belief in God, the Father of us all. I spoke of my faith in prayer, our avenue of communication with the Almighty, that blessed gift which makes it possible to reach out and tap that unseen Power we so much need. I testified that Jesus is the Christ; that he directs the course of this earth. I urged them to be unafraid, to love one another, to love all mankind, to pray for peace, and all would be well. I testified to the reality of the resurrection—that we are all eternal beings. I closed by leaving my witness as a church servant that truth will endure; that the basic concepts of Christianity are true, and that time is always on the side of truth. I invoked God's blessings upon them.

It has been my privilege to speak before many church bodies in all parts of the world, but the impact of that experience is almost indescribable. I have seldom, if ever, felt the oneness of humankind and the unquenchable yearning of the human heart for freedom more keenly than at that moment.

Ten members of the American press who were present felt it, too. Without exception they told me later what a moving experience it had been. Mr. Tom Anderson, editor of a farm magazine, wrote in the next issue of his magazine:

"These people have what has been described by some bubble-heads as 'freedom of religion.' It is freedom to live out their last few years without being shot in the back of the neck; freedom to go on existing in a living hell under a forced choice between God and their own families.

"These old souls live by faith alone, unlike the Communist high priests who're backed by the all-powerful state and the firing squad.

"The Communist plan is that when these 'last believers' die off, religion will die with them. What the atheists don't know is that God can't be stamped out either by legislated atheism or a firing squad. This Methodist back-slider who occasionally grumbles about having to go to church, stood crying unashamedly, throat lumped, and chills running from spine to toes. It was the most heart-rending and most inspiring scene I've ever witnessed.

"As we filed out they sang with all their hearts, 'God Be with You till We Meet Again.' And all knew we never would—on this earth. We also knew that some day, somehow, the greatest force in the world, love of God, will destroy this organized religion of hate.

"With heavy hearts we left to rejoin the smug, smart-aleck atheist guides who took us to the church but refused to go in.

"This trip with Secretary Benson was unforgettable. I was able to reach many conclusions, including the inscription I want for my tombstone: 'I'd rather be here than in Russia.' "

People do want peace—everywhere. People long to be free. In their hearts they yearn to be brothers.

I came home to this blessed land grateful for its blessings, humble in the face of responsibilities that confront us as free people—but filled with hope for the future, too.

I came back resolved to tell this story often—because it shows how the spirit of freedom, the spirit of brotherhood, and the spirit of religion live on and on even under immense difficulties.

With all my heart I love this great nation. I have lived and traveled abroad just enough to make me treasure what we have here. To me this is not just another nation, it is not just one of a family of nations. This is a nation with a great mission to perform for the benefit and blessing of liberty-loving people everywhere. It is my firm conviction that the Constitution of this land was established by men whom the God of heaven raised up unto this very purpose. Our land is to be a beacon of freedom—a testament to faith—a living witness to the fact of brotherhood.

Some day—in God's own due time—true brotherhood will come fully to life between nations. To speed that day, let us revivify its spirit in ourselves as individuals. Man to man let us act not just as acquaintances, nor even as friends—but as brothers.

God grant us wisdom and love so to do, I humbly pray.

(*Joint meetings of Salt Lake Rotary and Kiwanis Clubs and Chamber of Commerce, Salt Lake City, Utah, April 5, 1960.*)

Communist Threat to the Americas

In addressing you today, I take as my text these sober words of warning from an ancient American prophet:

"And others will he pacify, and lull them away into carnal security, that they will say: All is well in Zion; yea, Zion prospereth, all is well—and thus the devil cheateth their souls, and leadeth them away carefully down to hell.

"Therefore, wo be unto him that is at ease in Zion!

"Wo be unto him that crieth: All is well!"

(2 Nephi 28:21, 24, 25.)

We must not be deceived—all is not well.

We live today in an age of peril. It is an age in which we are threatened with the loss not only of wealth and material prosperity, but also of something far more precious —our freedom itself. The very thing that distinguishes man from the beasts—his freedom to act, freedom to choose, is threatened as never before by a total and atheistic philosophy of life known as communism.

In April, I called your attention briefly to the nature of communism. Let us remember these basic facts.

Those who subscribe to this philosophy stop at nothing to achieve their ends. They do not hesitate to destroy— if they are strong enough—whatever stands in their way. Our own generation has witnessed the Russian communists liquidate millions of their fellow countrymen. Even more recently we have seen the Chinese communists wipe out millions of their fellow countrymen—no one knows the exact number.

To the true communist, nothing is evil if it is expedient. Being without conscience or honor, he feels completely justified in using whatever means are necessary to achieve his goal: force, trickery, lies, broken promises, mayhem, and individual and mass murder.

By these ruthless means communism has, in a little over forty years, brought more people under its domination than the total number of Christians now living in the entire world—and Christianity, as the world thinks of it, has been in existence for nearly 2,000 years.

And what has been the result?

First in the economic area, men and women have been stripped of their property—their savings confiscated—their farms taken from them—their businesses seized by the state. They work where they are commanded to work and for such wages as the state chooses to provide. They cannot quit, take another job, or rebel in any tangible way. They are the puppets of the all-powerful state.

Second, in the intellectual area, they are forbidden to listen to radio broadcasts not approved by the state. They have little or no access to free world books, magazines, and newspapers. They have no voice in the education of their children in the schools. They and their children are cast in a communist mold. To write or speak against the state is to ask for exile, imprisonment, or possibly even death.

Third, in the area of morals, faith in moral principle is ruthlessly ridiculed and stripped of dignity. The belief that man has certain inalienable rights, so endowed by his Creator—is categorically denied. Atheistic communist leaders—scoffers at God himself—are striving to blot the Almighty out of the minds of one-third of the world's people.

To do all this, they rule with iron fists. They seek to hammer into oblivion all who would oppose them. Indeed it is true as the poet said:

> "Man's inhumanity to man
> Makes countless thousands mourn."

Let us have no illusions about them. Their leader has told us bluntly—their purpose is not alone to enslave us—they want to bury us.

And while it is apparently true that Chairman Khrushchev is content for the time being at least to avoid war as a means of communist expansion, there is little doubt that the leaders of Red China view war as inevitable and await only the propitious moment in which to strike.

What we face today is not just a cold war, not just a struggle for the control of land, sea, air, and even outer space, but total competition for the control of men's minds. Unless we meet it and defeat it, we shall almost inevitably one day face the loss of all that we hold dear.

In less than half a century, I repeat, this evil system has gained control over one-third of mankind, and it is steadily pursuing its vicious goal of control over all the rest of the world. It is time, and past time, for us to be alarmed. "Wo be unto him that is at ease. Wo be unto him that crieth 'all is well.'"

Latin America does not believe that suppression is the road to freedom.

True to communist and dictator tradition, the Cuban government has deprived its people of the rights of a free press, free elections, and the protection of other fundamental human rights.

And last August (1960) even as the Organization of American States met in San Jose, Costa Rica, Fidel Castro was shouting defiantly—"We shall be friends of the Soviet Union and the People's Republic of China."

How did this situation come about? How has it been possible for this completely warped philosophy in such a short time to reach its present position of influence in the world? How is it possible for communism to be here and now moving into Africa, pressing upon all of Asia, threatening the Middle East, and increasingly becoming a danger in the Western Hemisphere?

There are, of course, many reasons. Some nations have failed to provide for the advancement and desperate physical needs of their people. Others have failed to recognize the worth of the individual. But is it not perhaps true that the biggest reason of all is the failure of western civilization to live up to its Christian ideals?

Is it perhaps true that, as Dr. Charles Malik, the great Lebanese leader and former President of the United Nations General Assembly, has said,

"The deepest crisis of the West is the crisis of faith. . . . Western civilization is doomed until, jolted out of its complacency, self-satisfaction and sense of apartness, it rediscovers and reaffirms what is genuinely human and universal in its own soul?"

Let us examine into our own lives and the life of our own beloved land.

How richly we the people of the United States have been blessed!

Truly ours is a land of great favors and opportunities. Yet is it not true that these very blessings could prove to be our undoing unless our perspective is right and our idealism more concerned with eternal standards and values than with material gain and worldly honors?

How does our nation stand?

Are not many of us materialistic? Do we not find it well-nigh impossible to raise our sights above the dollar sign?

Are not many of us pragmatists—living not by principle but by what we can get away with?

Are not many of us status-seekers—measuring the worth of a man by the size of his bank account, his house, his automobile?

Are we not complacent, given to self-satisfaction, and self-congratulation—willing to co-exist with evil so long as it does not touch us personally.

If the answer to these questions is, yes—and who can honestly give a different answer?—then surely these are among the many reasons why this is truly an era of peril.

Many of us have a tendency to forget the Gracious Hand which has preserved our nation, enriched it, strengthened it. Many of us imagine in the foolishness of pride, that our manifold blessings are due not to God's goodness, but to our own wisdom and virtue. Too many of us have been so drunk with self-sufficiency as no longer to feel the need of prayer. Too many have forgotten the necessity of courage, of sacrifice, of vigilance, of devotion to the cause of freedom.

We must revivify western ideals and in particular the ideals of our own great nation. We must call back the spirit of the dauntless leaders of the past. We must meet our present-day challenge not with softness and complacency, but with the depth, wisdom, and daring that characterized America in the days of old.

The ancient American Prophet Moroni, saw our day. Who can doubt that he had in mind the evils of communism when he gave this solemn warning:

"Wherefore, O ye Gentiles, it is wisdom in God that these things should be shown unto you, that thereby ye may repent of your sins, and suffer not that these murderous combinations shall get above you, which are built up to get power and gain—and the work, yea, even the work of destruction come upon you, yea, even the sword of the justice of the Eternal God shall fall upon you, to your overthrow and destruction if ye shall suffer these things to be.

"Wherefore, the Lord commandeth you, when ye shall see these things come among you that ye shall awake to a sense of your awful situation, because of this secret combination which shall be among you; or wo be unto it, because of the blood of them who have been slain; for they cry from the dust for vengeance upon it, and also upon those who built it up.

"For it cometh to pass that whoso buildeth it up seeketh to overthrow the freedom of all lands, nations, and countries; and it bringeth to pass the destruction of all peo-

ple, for it is built up by the devil, who is the father of all lies."
(Ether 8:23-25.)

We are eminently justified in declaring that we should
consider any attempt on the part of the communists to extend their system to any part of this hemisphere as dangerous
to our peace and safety.

President Eisenhower said as much in his reply to the
tirade of Chairman Khrushchev last summer. But it is not
enough to say this once, nor is it enough for the President
alone to say it. It should be repeated again and again, and
it should be supported by all true Americans speaking as with
one voice.

In recent years the principles of the Monroe Doctrine
have been strengthened by various joint agreements among
the American nations.

In 1947, nineteen American nations met in conference
in Rio de Janeiro, and on September 2 of that year signed
the treaty of Rio de Janeiro in which they promised to help
one another in case of aggression.

On March 1, 1954, the Tenth Inter-American Conference opened in Caracas, Venezuela. When we read now,
six years later, the running account of that conference, it is
almost as though we were scanning a preview of history. On
March 4, for example, our late great Secretary of State, John
Foster Dulles, urged the American States to stop the communists now.

In March, the United States presented a draft resolution condemning communism as foreign intervention and
calling for joint action against it when needed.

On March 13, 1954, the conference adopted by a vote
of 17 to 1 the anti-communist resolution that had been presented by the United States. Guatemala dissented, and
Mexico and Argentina abstained.

Referring to the Caracas conference, President Eisenhower said, "In this hemisphere we have stressed our solid
understanding with our neighbors. . . . The American re-

publics agreed that if international communism were to gain control of the political institution of any American State, this control would endanger them all and therefore would demand collective action."

Very shortly after the close of the Caracas conference such a communist threat arose in Guatemala. The pro-communist government of Guatemala, aided by shipments of arms from behind the Iron Curtain, had moved very rapidly to the left. The Organization of American States had already convoked a meeting of foreign ministers under the Rio Treaty to consider the serious situation which had developed, when the Guatemalans themselves rose up and removed the threat. The meeting never convened. Fighting broke out in Guatemala, and the communist government was overthrown.

All this was before the coming to power of the present leadership in Cuba. Now the Western Hemisphere faces a new danger—a new threat.

Our government is alert to the situation. The Organization of American States has condemned Russian-Chinese interference in American affairs. These are first steps.

But we must do more. As a nation we must cease to take Latin American security for granted. We must lead this hemisphere in stimulating and co-operating in a program of Latin American economic development.

But even this is not enough. You and I and all true Americans must play our part, too.

What can you and I do? What can we do to help meet this grave challenge from a godless, atheistic, cruelly materialistic system—to preserve our God-given free way of life?

We can encourage our government to stand firm at all costs against any further expansion of communism into the free world.

We can tell our government that we are willing to

sacrifice our luxuries in exchange for an impregnable defense.

We can support our government in keeping the flame of freedom burning in the souls of the oppressed—wherever they may be throughout the world.

But, above all, we can face up to the decay in our own civilization.

The communists bring to the nations they infiltrate a message and a philosophy that affects human life in its entirety. Communists are willing to be revolutionary, to take a stand for this and against that. They challenge what they do not believe in—customs—practices—ideas—traditions. They believe *heatedly* in their philosophy.

But our civilization and our people are seemingly afraid to be revolutionary. We are too "broadminded" to challenge what we do not believe in. We are afraid of being thought intolerant—uncouth—ungentlemanly. We have become lukewarm in our beliefs.

This is a sad commentary on a civilization which has given to mankind the greatest achievements and progress known. But it is even sadder commentary on those of us who call ourselves Christians, who thus betray the ideals given to us by the Son of God himself.

Let us awaken to our responsibilities—and to our opportunities. Again I quote Dr. Malik.

"The civilization which has been blessed and transformed by Christ, needs only a mighty hand to shake it out of its slumber. And, once shaken, once really awakened to the world responsibilities which it and it alone can shoulder, there is nothing it cannot dare and do."

Do we believe that? Then let us live up to that faith! For in that faith—and through that faith—we can rise triumphant over the menace of atheistic communism—we can and we *must!*

In this dark hour, the fate of the world seems to rest largely in our hands. We who live in this choice land—in fact all of the land of Zion—have the opportunity, the responsibility, and the solemn obligation to stand firm for freedom and justice and morality—the dignity and brotherhood of man as a child of God.

"Wo be unto him that is at ease in Zion!
"Wo be unto him that crieth: All is well!"

(*Tabernacle, Salt Lake City, Utah, October Conference, 1960.*)

The Internal Threat to the American Way of Life

My Fellow Americans—

We are in the midst of continuing international crisis. The outlook for world peace and security is dark indeed. The gravity of the world situation is increasing almost daily. The United Nations seems unable to settle the troubles of the world. In truth we are faced with the hard fact that the United Nations seems to have largely failed in its purpose. Yes, the days ahead are sobering and challenging.

We live today in an age of peril. It is an age in which we are threatened with the loss not only of wealth and material prosperity, but also of something far more precious —our freedom itself. The very thing that distinguishes man from the beasts—his freedom to act, freedom to choose, is threatened as never before by a total and atheistic philosophy of life known as communism.

Never before in the history of our country has there been a greater need for all of our people to take a little time to discover what is happening in the world. Every day decisions are being made affecting the lives of millions of human beings. We now need, as much as during any crisis, the kind of courageous leadership which J. W. Hamilton called for when he said:

"How much now we need a leadership that will tell the truth and talk straight, not about what is expedient or even what is advantageous to American interests, but about what is everlastingly right, and call our people to a crusade for it, and pledge America to the defense of it, so that all nations will be convinced that we mean it! We need men who will ignore the consequences, tell the truth, and take a long chance with God." (*Ride the Wild Horses.*)

Such leadership must not be expected merely from those who serve in high offices. This is the kind of leadership we should be cultivating at every level—among parents, teachers, students, judges, the various professions, businessmen, laborers technicians, ministers—all of us need to join a crusade to develop men and women who talk straight, tell the truth and who are willing to take a course deserving of God's blessings.

A genuine leader tries to stay well informed. He is a person who acts on principle rather than expediency. He tries to learn from all human experience measured against revealed principles of divine wisdom. As a rule, a good leader is not easily deceived.

What has been lacking in our culture that has allowed the communists to deceive so many of our people so many different times? Perhaps part of it has been ignorance, another part misinformation and certainly an important part has been apathy-complacency. But whatever the lack has been, this is the kind of school (Freedom University of the Air) which is designed to do something about it.

Just a short time ago Fidel Castro broadcast to the world his boastful confession that he has been a hard-core communist all of his adult life. He gloried in the fact that he had been able to confuse and deceive many people simply by saying he was not a communist. And because there were people in this and other countries who believed his false assertions, he was able to establish a Soviet beachhead only ninety miles from our shores. Americans must face the cold hard fact that Fidel Castro was encouraged and supported in his seizure of Cuba. Why? Simply because many Americans were led to believe the falsehood that he would resist Soviet influence and restore the basic freedom of the Cuban people. A few of us issued early warnings based on unimpeachable evidence. Two United States ambassadors repeatedly warned that Castro was part of the communist camp and that he was working for the communist conquest of Cuba. These voices went unheeded.

This is merely a repetition of the same deceitful pattern which was used after World War II to have us tolerate revolutionary communists in China.

We are told that the high political officials in these countries, who surround themselves with known communist advisers, are merely trying to reconcile the various political factions and make their governments more representative. Later, after each country is taken over by the Fidel Castros, we are then assured that these men "betrayed the revolution." Research subsequently reveals that these men had been hard-core communists for many years.

Being without conscience or honor, the true communist feels completely justified in using whatever means are necessary to achieve his goal.

Let us have no illusions about them. Their leader has told us bluntly—their purpose is not alone to enslave us—they want to bury us.

What we face today is not just a cold war, not just a struggle for the control of land, sea, air, and even outer space, but total competition for the control of men's minds. Unless we meet it and defeat it, we shall almost inevitably one day face the loss of all that we hold dear.

In less than half a century this evil system has gained control over one-third of mankind and it is steadily pursuing its vicious goal of control over all the rest of the world. It is time, and past time, for us to be alarmed.

Latin America does not believe that suppression is the road to freedom.

Cuba is being used as a funnel through which communists are infiltrating other American republics.

Some nations have failed to provide for the advancement and desperate physical needs of their people. Others have failed to recognize the worth of the individual. But is it not perhaps true, that the biggest reason of all is the failure of western civilization to live up to its Judaic-Christian ideals?

We must revivify western ideals and in particular the ideals of our own great Nation. We must call back the spirit of the dauntless leaders of the past. We must meet our present-day challenge not with softness and complacency, but with the depth, wisdom, and daring that characterized America in the days of old.

The communists bring to the nations they infiltrate a message and a philosophy that affects human life in its entirety. Communism seeks to provide what in too many instances a lukewarm Christianity has not provided—a total interpretation of life. Communists challenge what they do not believe in—customs—practices—ideas—traditions. They believe heatedly in their philosophy.

But our civilization and our people are seemingly afraid to be revolutionary. We are too "broadminded" to challenge what we do not believe in. We are afraid of being thought intolerant—uncouth—ungentlemanly. We have become lukewarm in our beliefs. And for that we perhaps merit the bitter condemnation stated in the book of Revelation 3:16: "So then because thou art lukewarm, and neither cold nor hot, I will spue thee out of my mouth."

This is a sad commentary on a civilization which has given to mankind the greatest achievements and progress ever known. But it is even a sadder commentary on those of us who call ourselves Christians, who thus betray the ideals given to us by the Son of God himself. Again, I ask, are we going to permit the atheistic communist masters, fellow travelers, and dupes to deceive us any longer?

There is a deception going on in our country this very moment which is just as dangerous to the United States as the false pretensions of Fidel Castro were to Cuba. It is amazing to me that some of our citizens seem to take special delight in ridiculing the warnings of government investigators and the cry of alarm which comes from Iron Curtain refugees when they see how the United States is being led carefully down the trail of disaster.

Clear back in 1953 the Jenner Committee published a report on June 30 of that year which should have sobered the entire country. This report stated:

"1. The Soviet international organization has carried on a successful and important penetration of the United States Government and this penetration has not fully been exposed.

2. This penetration has extended from the lower ranks to top-level policy and operating positions in our government.

3. The agents of this penetration have operated in accordance with a distinct design fashioned by their Soviet superiors.

4. Members of the conspiracy helped to get each other into government, helped each other to rise in government, and protected each other from exposure. (The 1st Communist Cell in government was organized in the U.S. Dept. of agriculture in the 1930's.)

* * * * *

6. In general, the communists who infiltrated our government worked behind the scenes—guiding research and preparing memoranda on which basic American policies were set, writing speeches for Cabinet officers, influencing congressional investigations, drafting laws, manipulating administrative reorganization—always serving the interests of their Soviet superiors.

* * * * *

12. Policies and programs laid down by members of this Soviet conspiracy are still in effect within our government, and constitute a continuing hazard in our national security."

Eleven years have passed since that warning was given, but the American people have not yet insisted upon the housecleaning which is so long overdue. In this year, 1961, that fearless and distinguished American, J. Edgar Hoover, testified before the House Appropriations committee and said:

"The Soviet intelligence services have reorganized, multiplied their contacts with the American people, and have become aggressively bolder in spearheading their espionage offensive against the United States." (FBI Appropriation Hearing, March 6, 1961, p. 49.)

Speaking of communist front organizations, he said:

"They represent transmission belts through which the Communist Party furthers its conspiratorial designs. They have infiltrated every conceivable sphere of activity: youth groups; radio, television, and motion picture industries, Church, school, education and cultural groups; the press, nationality minority groups and civil and political units." (*Idem.*)

Of course, such groups can have only one purpose and that is deception. The only way to avoid being deceived is to get the facts. Here are people who would try to hide the facts from us and replace the truth with a falsehood. They want us to believe that America is a failure, that her system of capitalistic free-enterprise is doomed, that she must remedy her failures by adopting Marxist theories of collectivized control. I recognize these voices. I heard them in 43 nations which I visited in the past few years. I heard them often during my eight years in Washington. None of them came to me in the name of communism or even socialism, but they came. And while many of us fought them and resisted them on every front, nevertheless, it was alarming to discover how many others were willing to believe and follow. Why do otherwise loyal Americans believe and follow? Because these voices came from masters of deception.

Now suppose a person came along and said, "I am in favor of doing away with competitive markets and private property, of setting communes in each locality, of taking all the land away from the farmers, of taking over all the steel mills, all the electric power plants, all the automotive industry, the banks, the railroads, the newspapers, the television and radio stations, all the mines, and so forth." I am sure such a proposal would meet with immediate and united resistance by the vast majority of the American people. But suppose this same person came and said: "It is in the public interest and to the benefit of each citizen if we make industry, the farms, and all means of production and distribution operate for the benefit of all the people and not just for the private profit of a few stockholders." Immediately this line of deception receives a wave of support. It is occurring today here in the United States. It occurred in England, France, and Eastern Europe as well as the Scandinavian countries. It occurred in Russia.

If you ask the individual who made this last statement whether or not he is a communist or socialist, he will undoubtedly reply with great indignation that he is a loyal American—that he is very anti-communist. He will generally say he merely wants to see our nation achieve marvelous new goals which will make our present standard of living appear meager indeed. When you ask this individual where his plan has been tried and proved successful, he will tell you it is a plan of the future, and its virtues are yet to be demonstrated. And if you press him even further by pointing out that his program sounds exactly like the Marxist socialism of Europe he may become extremely indignant and call you a "reactionary" who doesn't want to see the country progress.

Now this accusation, of course, is as false as it is unfair. All of us are anxious to see our country progress, but we want to know by what means. The whole American concept of progress, which has outstripped every other nation on earth, is based on certain fundamental principles which these men now ask us to abandon. Certainly we are entitled to challenge such proposals when they are asking us to give up what has worked so well and substitute something which they merely hope will work.

What are these fundamental principles which have allowed the United States to progress so rapidly and yet remain free?

First, a written Constitution clearly defining the limits of government so that government will not become more powerful than the people.

Second, a sound economic system.

Third, building an open society where each individual enjoys the greatest opportunity to improve himself, to travel, to become educated, to invent, to compete, to build, to speak, to worship, and to pursue happiness in whatever way the individual finds most satisfying and worthwhile.

Fourth, assigning government the role of referee rather than competitor—giving it enough power to provide peace, order and security but not enough power to rob the people of their liberty or take away their property "without due process of law."

Of course, it immediately becomes apparent that if certain people wanted to seize control of private property, if they wanted to nationalize the land, if they wanted to have the government take over all the industries, the schools, the transportation complex and communications network, the way to do it would be by "due process of law." Therefore, certain people have set out to do this very thing.

Is this possible? It is indeed, and every American should know it. As the Marxist socialists declared over seventy years ago: "Convert the electorate and capture the

County Councils." (*Fabian Essays on Socialism,* Doubleday & Co., New York, 1960, p. 190.) More recently Khrushchev has emphasized the same thing. In 1956 he said:

"In this connection the question arises of whether it is possible to go over to socialism by using parliamentary means. . . . The forces of socialism and democracy have grown immeasurably throughout the world, and capitalism has become much weaker. . . . In these circumstances the working class, by rallying around itself the toiling peasantry, the intelligentsia, all patriotic forces . . . is in a position to defeat the reactionary forces opposed to the popular interest, to capture a stable majority in parliament, and transform the latter from an organ of bourgeois democracy into a genuine instrument of the people's will. . . ." (House Committee on Un-American Activities, *Facts on Communism,* Vol. I, pp. 114-115.)

What Khrushchev is talking about is what he calls "peaceful victory of socialism," or seizing the natural and human resources of the earth "by due process of law."

He is not alone in this ambition. In this project he is paralleling the position of another branch of Marxism which might be called the social democrats since this is the name they took in Russia and most of Europe. Lenin himself helped to organize the Social Democratic Party in Russia but in 1903 he set up his own branch of the party and called them Bolsheviks which became the vanguard of revolutionary violence in the party.

But notice what happened in Russia. It was the social democrats, or the ones who wanted to seize power "by due process of law" who organized the original soviets, who concentrated the power over the industrial workers into a few hands, who overthrew the czar, and who set up conditions in Russia from March to October, 1917, which made it possible for the communists or Bolsheviks to move in with force and violence and take over Russia in November 1917. Notice that the social democrats did their organizing in the name of the welfare of the people. After they had provided the basic concentration of power, the forces of Lenin seized control, and the people found themselves under the harsh cruelty of a communist dictatorship.

This is a most important lesson for all of us to learn, namely, that the communists use the socialists to pave the way for them wherever possible. This is why communists and socialists are often found supporting each other, collaborating together, and fighting for the same goals.

The paramount issue today is freedom against creeping socialism. The well-known British writer, John Strachey, who for many years was an openly avowed communist and who served as Minister of War in the socialist government in 1950, made this very plain in his book, *The Theory and Practice of Socialism*. Said he:

"It is impossible to establish Communism as the immediate successor to capitalism. It is, accordingly, proposed to establish Socialism as something which we can put in the place of our present decaying capitalism. Hence, Communists work for the establishment of Socialism as a necessary transition stage on the road to Communism." (John Strachey, *The Theory and Practice of Socialism*, Random House, New York, 1936, p. 121.)

Now obviously, the worst thing that can happen to a socialist is to have himself openly identified with the work of the communists who are generally feared and despised. The socialists know they cannot seize property and power by "due process of law" unless they are politically popular, therefore, they try desperately to avoid the taint of the communists and present their program so that it appears "moral," "democratic," "peaceful," and so "gradual" that the people will not resist it.

These are the exact words used by the social democrats in England in 1889 (*Fabian Essays on Socialism*, Doubleday & Co. New York, 1960, p. 51), when they were preparing to lay the foundation for the seizure of power which finally took place after World War I and again after World War II. They prepared a book called *"Fabian Essays on Socialism."* In the preface they said the book was being written by seven members of the executive council of the Fabian Society. They then said, "The writers are all Social Democrats." Nevertheless, they adopted the name of "Fabians" after the Roman General, Fabius, who won his battles by capturing or defeating the enemy a few at a time. This is what the social democrats call "gradualism." It is their intention to use this method in conquering their enemies which in this case happens to be free men.

Here is what these Fabians or social democrats said they were going to do:

With reference to private property they said: ". . . private property in land and capital will inevitably go the way of feudalism which it superseded." (Idem.)

The social democrats also said they were going to work for "the ultimate and gradual extinction of the (property-owning) class." (*Idem.*)

They said they were going to nationalize or collectivize the land. They described how they would set up collectivized farms. They would organize communes in each locality. They would get clothes from a community store, eat at a community table the food prepared in a community kitchen. They would nationalize the major industries and develop industrial communes for the smaller industries. (*Ibid.*, especially pp. 184-185, 190-196.)

At this point some of you may wonder whether I am talking about communism in Russia rather than the social democrats in England. But I have mentioned these things so that you can see that in their final form the two are identical.

The Fabians even recognize the problem of compulsory labor which might be necessary under their system. In fact, within one year after the British Fabians had seized power and socialized the major industries following World War II, they found it necessary to impose controlled or compulsory labor management on the workers. But compulsion was nothing new in the thinking of social democrats. One of their original founders emphasized this when he said:

"I also made it quite clear that under Socialism you would not be allowed to be poor. You would be forcibly fed, clothed, lodged, taught and employed whether you liked it or not. If it were discovered that you had not character and industry enough to be worth all this trouble, you might possibly be executed in a kindly manner; but whilst you were permitted to live you would have to live well." (George B. Shaw, *Intelligent Woman's Guide to Socialism and Capitalism*, p. 470.)

The social democrats even described the serf-like existence of the workers under their program. They pointed out that "the perfect fitting development of each individual is not necessarily the utmost and highest cultivation of his own personality, but the filling, in the best possible way, of his humble function in the great social machines." (*Fabian Essays on Socialism*, Doubleday & Co., New York, 1960, p. 79.)

One final observation concerning the socialist plan to seize power by "due process of law." During the gradual seizure of land and property there will still be some private industry operating. They describe how they will gradually smother and destroy it. Here is what they say about this stage of their take-over:

"The private capitalist, however, will still be in business, producing and distributing on his own account in competition with the communal organization, which at present will have occupied only part of the industrial field.

But . . . these private enterprises will be carried on under circumstances of ever-increasing difficulty."

They then describe how the government-owned industries, operating with government credit behind them, will begin to choke off private enterprise. They say, "After a while the private producers will disappear, not because there will be any law against individualist production, but because they will not pay." (*Ibid.*, p. 195.)

All of this may begin to sound familiar to many American businessmen who have been watching similar influences of creeping socialism gradually using government regulations or government ownership to destroy the basic framework of economic freedom and private production in our own country.

We must ever keep in mind that collectivized socialism is part of the communist strategy. Communism is fundamentally socialism. We will never win our fight against communism by making concessions to socialism. Communism and socialism must be defeated on principle.

When socialism is understood, we will realize that many of the programs advocated, and some of those already adopted in the United States, fall clearly within the category of socialism. What is socialism? It is simply governmental ownership and management of the essential means for the production and distribution of goods.

We must never forget that nations may sow the seeds of their own destruction while enjoying unprecedented prosperity.

The socialistic communist conspiracy to weaken the United States involves attacks on many fronts. To weaken the American free-enterprise economy which outproduced both its enemies and allies during World War II, is a high priority target of the communist leaders. Their press and other propaganda media are therefore constantly selling the principles of centralized or federal control of farms, railroads, electric power, schools, steel, maritime shipping, and many other aspects of the economy—but always in the name of public welfare.

For thirty years we have aided the cause of atheistic, socialistic communism by permitting communists in high places in government; by giving away vital military secrets; by squandering much of our material resources; by recklessly spending ourselves to near bankruptcy; by weakening our free enterprise system through adoption of socialistic policies; by wasteful bungling of our foreign affairs; by ever-increasing confiscatory taxation and by permitting the insidious infiltration of communist agents and sympathizers into almost every segment of American life.

Many people have wondered if the Marxist concepts of the Fabian social democrats have deeply penetrated the United States. In truth they have. British social democrats came to the United States in 1888 for a long visit to train Fabian groups in several of the leading universities. Eventually their followers were organized into the Intercollegiate Socialist Society in 1905. By 1916 this organization was becoming increasingly influential and its members were already climbing into the higher echelons of the government. After World War I the society changed its name to the League for Industrial Democracy and continued to plant its most brilliant personalities in government, education, communications and policy making bodies. There they remain today, occupying some of the highest offices in the land. Their records will show that they have consistently sponsored the basic ideas of the social democrats of Europe. Some of them have been exposed, as not only being sympathetic, and collaborating with their fellow Marxists of the USSR, but actually joining them.

This, then, brings me to my final point, namely, that the internal threat to the American way of life is in the secret alliance which exists between the more advanced social democrats and the hard-core communist conspiracy.

Occasionally this sympathetic alliance breaks out into the open but most of the time it is maintained in the labyrinths of quiet secrecy. If you should wonder why socialists in this and other countries have often played into the hands of world communism you might consider these words from the top British socialist, G. D. H. Cole, who wrote the following words during World War II:

"I have never allowed my dislike of much that Stalin has done to blind me to the fact that the USSR remains fundamentally Socialist, or that the Soviet form of revolution and of government may be the only one that is capable of sweeping clean the stables of Eastern and Southern Europe, or of solving the basic economic problems of the unhappy peasants of these impoverished States. . . . I am ready to go further. I would much sooner the Soviet Union, even with its policy unchanged, became dominant over all Europe, including Great Britain, than see an attempt to restore the pre-war States to their futile and uncreative independence and their petty economic nationalism under capitalistic domination. Much better be ruled by Stalin than by the restrictive and monopolistic cliques which dominate Western capitalism."

Mr. Cole concludes by saying, "For it would be much better to live within a system, however barbaric in some of its features, that has in it some creative force making for the liberation of mankind from class-oppression and primary poverty than to thrust back under the dead hand of decaying capitalism utterly incapable of fresh, creative effort." (G. D. H. Cole, *Europe, Russia and the Future*, Macmillan Co., New York, 1942, pp. 8-9.)

It would appear to me that when a mind has been trained to hold such bitterness against capitalism; to believe so blindly in the illusions of communism, it is no wonder that some of this preceding mentality have used their influence in scientific circles, in embassies and in governmental positions to betray the interests of their own countries and collaborate with what has turned out to be the most formidable enemy free men have ever faced.

I believe J. Edgar Hoover and the investigating committees of Congress know whereof they speak when they warn us of a serious internal threat to the American way of life. I hear that some people and more particularly the communists and the social democrats don't want us to examine this internal threat, but I believe we should. I think we should study communism and study socialism so we can recognize the influence of each. We can leave the spies to the FBI, but learning how our enemies are trying to subvert us is everybody's job. I also recognize that it is not popular in some circles to be called an anti-communist, but I consider communism a godless political and economic disease. I do not believe an American citizen can be patriotic and loyal to his own country, and its God-inspired Constitution, of freedom, without being anti-communist.

Now I know that Moscow has ordered that all anti-communists are to be attacked and discredited in every way possible. I know the Communist Party of the United States has issued a similar mandate. This does not disturb me at all. It should be expected. Meanwhile we should pursue a calm and steady course. We should expose to the light of public inquiry those forces which would destroy our country and our way of life. We should pay no attention to the recommendations of men who call the Constitution an eighteenth century agrarian document—who apologize for capitalism and free enterprise. We should refuse to follow their siren song of concentrating, increasingly, the powers of government in the Chief Executive, of delegating American sovereign authority to non-American institutions in the United Nations, and pretending that it will bring peace to the world by turning our armed forces over to a U.N. world-wide police force.

My own political and economic creed is a simple one. I commend it to you:

I am for freedom and against slavery.

I am for social progress and against socialism.

I am for a dynamic economy and against waste.

I am for the private competitive market and against unnecessary government intervention.

I am for private ownership and against governmental ownership and control of the means of production and distribution.

I am for national security and against appeasement and capitulation to an obvious enemy.

This contest in which we are engaged is as old as man and as young as hope. The issue is over the God-given eternal principle of freedom—free agency, the right of choice. In this struggle it is not enough to be right—we must put strength and action back of that which is right.

In the conflict with socialistic communism we must have patience, courage, and wisdom. We must also have friends. Russia has hostages—we have friends—millions of them in temporary slavery back of the iron curtain, and millions more to be mobilized throughout the free world. In Russia people are unable to challenge the despotic godless dogmas forced on the people. We must take greater risks for freedom. We must dramatize "American might and Soviet myth."

Let us awaken to our responsibilities—and to our opportunities.

I love America. I know you do. God and our children will judge us for what we do with our land and our liberties. As Theodore Roosevelt said over half a century ago, we "hold in our hands the hope of the world, the fate of the coming years, and shame and disgrace will be ours if in our eyes the light of high resolve is dimmed, if we trail in the dust the golden hopes of men."

With God's help the light of high resolve in the eyes
of the American people must never be dimmed. Our freedom
must—and will be preserved.

May God give us the wisdom to recognize the threat
to our freedom and the strength to meet this danger
courageously.

(Shrine Auditorium, Los Angeles, California, December 11, 1961.)

The American Heritage of Freedom —
A Plan of God

My theme is directed particularly to the men of America and more especially to those in The Church of Jesus Christ of Latter-day Saints who hold the Holy Priesthood of God.

Every member of the priesthood should understand the divine plan designed by the Lord to raise up the first free people in modern times. Here is how scripture says it was achieved:

First: Prophecy is abundant that God deliberately kept the American continent hidden until after the Holy Roman Empire had been broken up and the various nations had established themselves as independent kingdoms. Keeping America hidden until this time was no accident. (2 Nephi 1:6, 8.)

Second: At the proper time, God inspired Columbus to overcome almost insurmountable odds to discover America and bring this rich new land to the attention of the gentiles in Europe. (1 Nephi 13:12; Dr. Samuel Eliot Morison, *Admiral of the Ocean Sea*, pp. 46-47.)

Third: God revealed to his ancient American prophets that shortly after the discovery of America there would be peoples in Europe who would desire to escape the persecution and tyranny of the Old World and flee to America. (1 Nephi 13:13-16.)

Fourth: God told his prophets that the kingdoms in Europe would try to exercise dominion over the people who had fled to America, but that in the wars for independence the American settlers would win. (This is a remarkable prophecy in that 2,300 years before the Revolutionary War was fought, God through his prophets predicted who would win it.) (*Ibid.*, 16-19.)

Fifth: The prophets were told that in the latter days when the gentiles came to America they would establish it as a land of liberty on which there would be no kings. The Lord declared that he would protect the land and whosoever would try to establish kings either from within or without should perish. (2 Nephi 10:8-14.)

Sixth: Having declared America to be a land of liberty, God undertook to raise up a band of inspired and intelligent leaders who could write a constitution of liberty and establish the first free people in modern times. The hand of God in this undertaking is clearly indicated by the Lord, himself, in a revelation to the Prophet Joseph Smith in these words:

". . . I established the Constitution of this land, by the hands of wise men whom I raised up unto this very purpose. . . ." (Doctrine & Covenants 101:80.)

Seventh: God declared that the United States Constitution was divinely inspired for the specific purpose of eliminating bondage and the violation of the rights and protection which belong to "all flesh." (*Ibid.*, 77-80.)

Eighth: God placed a mandate upon his people to befriend and defend the constitutional laws of the land and see that the rights and privileges of all mankind are protected. He verified the declaration of the founding fathers that God created all men free. He also warned against those who would enact laws encroaching upon the sacred rights and privileges of free men. He urged the election of honest and wise leaders and said that evil men and laws were of Satan. (*Ibid.*, 98:5-10.)

Ninth: God predicted through his prophets that this great gentile nation, raised upon the American continent in the last days, would become the richest and most powerful on the face of the earth; even "above all other nations." (1 Nephi 13:15, 30; Ether 2:12.)

Tenth: Concerning the United States, the Lord revealed to his prophets that its greatest threat would be a vast, world-wide "secret combination" which would not only threaten the United States but seek to "overthrow the freedom of all lands, nations, and countries." (Ether 8:25.)

Eleventh: In connection with the attack on the United States, the Lord told the Prophet Joseph Smith there would be an attempt to overthrow the country by destroying the Constitution. Joseph Smith predicted that the time would come when the Constitution would hang as it were by a thread, and at that time, "this people will step forth and save it from the threatened destruction." (*Journal History,* July 4, 1854.)

It is my conviction that the elders of Israel, widely spread over the nation, will, at the crucial time, successfully rally the righteous of our country and provide the necessary balance of strength to save the institutions of constitutional government.

Twelfth: The Lord revealed to the Prophet Nephi that he established the gentiles on this land to be a free people forever, that if they were a righteous nation and overcame the wickedness and secret abominations which would arise in their midst, they could inherit the land forever. (1 Nephi 14:1-2.)

Thirteenth: But on the other hand, if the gentiles on this land reject the word of God and conspire to overthrow the liberty and the Constitution, then their doom is fixed, and they "shall be cut off from among my people who are of the covenant." (3 Nephi 21:11, 14, 21; 1 Nephi 14:6; D&C 84:114, 115, 117.)

Fourteenth: The great destructive force which was to be turned loose on the earth and which the prophets for centuries have been calling the "abomination of desolation" is vividly described by those who saw it in vision. Ours is the first generation to realize how literally these prophecies can be fulfilled now that God, through science, has unlocked the secret to thermonuclear reaction.

In the light of these prophecies there should be no doubt in the mind of any priesthood holder that the human family is headed for trouble. There are rugged days ahead. It is time for every man who wishes to do his duty to get himself prepared—physically, spiritually, and psychologically—for the task which may come at any time, as suddenly as the whirlwind.

Where do we stand today? All over the world the light of freedom is being diminished. Across whole continents of the earth freedom is being totally obliterated.

Never in recorded history has any movement spread its power so far and so fast as has socialistic-communism in the last three decades. The facts are not pleasant to review. Communist leaders are jubilant with their success. They are driving freedom back on almost every front.

It is time, therefore, that every American, and especially every member of the priesthood became informed about the aims, tactics, and schemes of socialistic-communism. This becomes particularly important when it is realized that communism is turning out to be the earthly image of the plan which Satan presented in the pre-existence. The whole program of socialistic-communism is essentially a war against God and the plan of salvation—the very plan which we fought to uphold during "the war in heaven."

Up to now some members of the Church have stood aloof, feeling that the fight against socialistic-communism is "controversial" and unrelated to the mission of the Church or the work of the Lord. But the President of the Church in our day has made it clear that the fight against atheistic communism is a major challenge to the Church and every member of it.

During the general conference of the Church in October, 1959, President David O. McKay, in discussing the threat of communism, referred to W. Cleon Skousen's book *The Naked Communist* and said, "I admonish everybody to read that excellent book." He then quoted the following from the flyleaf: "The conflict between communism and freedom is the problem of our time. It overshadows all other problems."

The fight against godless communism is a very real part of every man's duty who hold the priesthood. It is the fight against slavery, immorality, atheism, terrorism, cruelty, barbarism, deceit, and the destruction of human life through a kind of tyranny unsurpassed by anything in human history. Here is a struggle against the evil, satanical priestcraft of Lucifer. Truly it can be called, "a continuation of the war in heaven."

In the war in heaven the devil advocated absolute eternal security at the sacrifice of our freedom. Although there is nothing more desirable to a Latter-day Saint than eternal security in God's presence, and although God knew, as did we, that some of us would not achieve this security if we were allowed our freedom—yet the very God of heaven, who has more mercy than us all, still decreed no guaranteed security except by a man's own freedom of choice and individual initiative.

Today the devil as a wolf in a supposedly new suit of sheep's clothing is enticing some men, both in and out of the Church, to parrot his line by advocating planned government guaranteed security programs at the expense of our liberties. Latter-day Saints should be reminded how and why they voted as they did in heaven. If some have decided to change their vote, they should repent—throw their support on the side of freedom—and cease promoting this subversion.

When all of the trappings of propaganda and pretense have been pulled aside, the exposed hard-core structure of modern communism is amazingly similar to the ancient Book of Mormon record of secret societies such as the Gadiantons. In the ancient American civilization there was no word which struck greater terror in the hearts of the people than the name of the Gadiantons. It was a secret political party which operated as a murder cult. Its object was to infiltrate legitimate government, plant its officers in high places, and then seize power and live off the spoils appropriated from the people. (It would start out as a small group of "dissenters" and by using secret oaths with the threat of death for defectors it would gradually gain a choke hold on the political and economic life of whole civilizations.)

The object of the Gadiantons, like modern communists, was to destroy the existing government and set up a ruthless criminal dictatorship over the whole land.

One of the most urgent, heart-stirring appeals made by Moroni as he closed the Book of Mormon was addressed to the gentile nations of the last days. He foresaw the rise of a great world-wide secret combination among the gentiles which "*seeketh to overthrow the freedom of all lands, nations, and countries; . . .*" He warned each gentile nation of the last days to purge itself of this gigantic criminal conspiracy which would seek to rule the world.

The prophets, in our day, have continually warned us of these internal threats in our midst—that our greatest threat from socialistic-communism lies within our country. We don't need a prophet—we have one—we need a listening ear. And if we do not listen and heed, then, as the Doctrine and Covenants states, ". . . the day cometh that they who will not hear the voice of the Lord, neither the voice of his servants, neither give heed to the words of the prophets and apostles, shall be cut off from among the people;" (D&C 1:14.)

The prophets have said that these threats are among us. The Prophet Moroni viewing our day said, "Wherefore, the Lord commandeth you, when ye shall see these things come among you that ye shall awake to a sense of your awful situation. . . ." (Ether 8:24.)

Unfortunately our nation has not treated the socialistic-communist conspiracy as "treasonable to our free institutions," as the First Presidency pointed out in a signed 1936 statement. If we continue to uphold communism, by not making it treasonable, our land shall be destroyed, for the Lord has said ". . . whatsoever nation shall uphold such secret combinations, to get power and gain, until they shall spread over the nation, behold they shall be destroyed; . . ." (*Ibid.*, 8:22.)

The Prophet Moroni described how the secret combination would take over a country and then fight the work of God, persecute the righteous and murder those who resisted. Moroni therefore proceeded to describe the working of the ancient "secret combinations" so that modern man could recognize this great political conspiracy in the last days. Said he: "Wherefore, O ye Gentiles, it is wisdom in God that these things should be shown unto you, that thereby ye may repent of your sins, and suffer not these murderous combinations shall get above you, which are built up to get power and gain—and the work, yea, even the work of destruction come upon you, . . .

"Wherefore, the Lord commandeth you, when ye shall see these things come among you that ye shall awake to a sense of your awful situation, because of this secret combination which shall be among you; . . .

"For it cometh to pass that whoso buildeth it up seeketh to overthrow the freedom of all lands, nations, and countries; and it bringeth to pass the destruction of *all* people, for it is built up by the devil, who is the father of all lies; . . ." (*Ibid.*, 8:23-25.)

The Prophet Moroni seemed greatly excited lest in our day we might not be able to recognize the startling fact that the same secret societies which destroyed the Jaredites and decimated numerous kingdoms of both Nephites and Lamanites would be precisely the same form of criminal conspiracy which would rise up among the gentile nations in this day.

The stratagems of the leaders of these societies are amazingly familiar to anyone who has studied the tactics of modern communist leaders.

The Lord has declared that before the second coming of Christ it will be necessary to "destroy the secret works of darkness," in order to preserve the land of Zion—the Americas. (2 Nephi 10:11-16.)

The world-wide secret conspiracy which has risen up in our day to fulfil these prophecies is easily identified. President McKay has left no room for doubt as to what attitude Latter-day Saints should take toward the modern "secret combination" of conspiratorial communism. In a lengthy statement on communism, he said:

". . . *Latter-day Saints should have nothing to do with the secret combinations* and groups antagonistic to the constitutional law of the land, which the Lord 'suffered to be established,' and which 'should be maintained for the rights and protection of all flesh according to just and holy principles.'" (*Gospel Ideals,* by David O. McKay, p. 306.)

There are those who recommend that the clash between communism and freedom be avoided through disarmament agreements. Abolishing our military strength and adopting an unenforceable contract as a substitute to protect us would go down in history as the greatest mistake free men could make in a time of peril.

President McKay declared:

"Force rules in the world today; consequently, our government must keep armies abroad, build navies and

air squadrons, create atom bombs to protect itself from the
threatened aggression of a nation which seems to listen
to no other appeal than compulsion." (*Ibid.*, p. 304.)

This statesmanlike statement parallels the historic
statement by George Washington when he vigorously
warned:

"There is a rank due the United States among nations
that will be totally lost by the reputation of weakness. If
we would avoid insult, we must be able to repel it; if we
would secure the peace, it must be known that we are at
all times ready for war."

Some timid, vacillating political leaders proclaim that
communism is something we will have to learn to live with
. . . whether it is Khrushchev, or some other leader. The
present communist system, they declare, will continue because *there is no alternate system to replace communism.*
The policy of increasing power, of pushing their system
outward and using the communist party, they say, will
go on.

Such a negative attitude writes off the hundreds of
millions behind the iron curtain as a lost cause. Surely no
courageous, liberty-loving citizens will treat the communist
secret combination as "something we will have to learn
to live with."

There is a more courageous and sounder point of view.
President McKay expressed it in these words:

"Men will be free. I have hoped for twenty years that
the Russian system would break up. There is no freedom
under it, and *sooner or later the people will rise against it.*
They cannot oppose those fundamentals of civilization and
of God. They can't crush their people always. Men will
be free." (Church Section, *Deseret News*, November 6,
1957, in an article entitled, "President McKay Receives
Senator Kennedy at Church Offices.")

What is the official position of the Church on communism? In 1936 the First Presidency made an official declaration on communism which has never been abrogated. I quote the concluding paragraph:

"We call upon all Church members completely to eschew communism. The safety of our divinely inspired constitutional government and the welfare of our Church imperatively demand that communism shall have no place in America."

We must ever keep in mind that collectivized socialism is part of the communist strategy. Communism is fundamentally socialism. Communism and socialism closely related, must be defeated on principle. The close relationship between socialism and communism is clearly pointed out by Senator Strom Thurmond of South Carolina in a letter to the editor of the Washington *Post*, of August 6, 1961, in these words:

"Both socialism and communism derive from the teachings of Marx and Engels. In fact, the movements were one until the split over methods of approach, which resulted after the Russian revolution in 1905. . . . The aim and purpose of both was then and is now world socialism, which communism seeks to achieve through revolution and which socialists seek to achieve through evolution.

"The industrial achievements of the U.S. are the result of an economic system which is the antithesis of socialism. Our economic system is called capitalism or private enterprise and is based on private property rights, the profit motive and competition.

"Both communism and socialism seek to destroy our economic system and replace it with socialism; and their success, whether through evolution by socialism or through revolution by communism, or a combination, will destroy not only our economic system, but our liberty, including the 'civil' aspects as well. . . .

". . . The 'common ground' of socialism and communism is a factor to which the American people should be alerted. Without a clear understanding in that communism is socialism, the total threat and menace of the cold war can never be comprehended and fought to victory."

When socialism is understood, we will realize that many of the programs advocated, and some of those already adopted in the United States, fall clearly within the category of socialism. What is socialism? It is simply governmental ownership and management of the essential means for the production and distribution of goods.

We must never forget that nations may sow the seeds of their own destruction while enjoying unprecedented prosperity.

The socialistic-communist conspiracy to weaken the United States involves attacks on many fronts. Their press and other propaganda media are therefore constantly selling the principles of centralized or federal control of farms, railroads, electric power, schools, steel, maritime shipping and many other aspects of the economy—but always in the name of public welfare.

This carries out the strategy laid down by the communist masters. John Strachey, a top official in the Labor Socialist party of Great Britain, in his book entitled *The Theory and Practice of Socialism* said:

"It is impossible to establish Communism as the immediate successor to Capitalism. It is accordingly proposed to establish Socialism as something which we can put in the place of our present decaying Capitalism. Hence, Communists work for the establishment of Socialism as a necessary transition stage on the road to Communism."

The paramount issue today is liberty against creeping socialism. It is in this spirit that President McKay stated:

"Communism is antagonistic to the American way of life. Its avowed purpose is to destroy belief in God and *free enterprise.* . . . The fostering of full economic freedom lies at the base of our liberties. Only in perpetuating economic freedom can our social, political, and religious liberties be preserved."

(Excerpt from Inaugural address for Dr. Henry A. Dixon, Pres. of U.S.U, delivered by President McKay, at the USU fieldhouse, Logan, Utah, 3-8-54.)

Again President McKay warned,

"During the first half of the twentieth century we have traveled far into the soul-destroying land of socialism and made strange alliances through which we have become involved in almost continuous hot and cold war over the whole of the earth. In this retreat from freedom the voices of protesting citizens have been drowned by raucous shouts of intolerance and abuse from those who led the retreat and their millions of gullible youth, who are marching merrily to their doom, carrying banners on which are emblazoned such intriguing and misapplied labels as social justice, equality, reform, patriotism, social welfare." (*Gospel Ideals*, by David O. McKay, p. 273.)

It is significant to me that 120 years ago the Prophet Joseph Smith after attending lectures on socialism, made this official entry in Church history: "I said I did not believe the doctrine." (*History of the Church*, Vol. 6, p. 33.)

No true Latter-day Saint and no true American can be a socialist or a communist or support programs leading in that direction. These evil philosophies are incompatible with Americanism, with Mormonism, and with the true gospel of Jesus Christ.

What can priesthood holders do? There are many things we can do to meet the challenge of the adversary in our day.

First, we should become informed about communism, about socialism, and about Americanism. What better way can one become informed than by first studying the inspired words of the prophets and using them as a foundation against which to test all other material. This is in keeping with the Prophet Joseph Smith's motto, "When the Lord commands, do it." (*Ibid.*, Vol. II, p. 170.)

The Foundation for Economic Education, Irvington-on-Hudson, New York, on which President J. Reuben Clark served as a board member, continues to supply sound freedom literature. We should know enough about American free enterprise to be able to defend it. We should know what makes it possible for six percent of humanity—living under our free economy—to produce about one-half of the earth's developed wealth each year.

We should know why paternalism, collectivism, or unnecessary federal supervision will hold our standard of living down and reduce productivity just as it has in every country where it has been tried. We should also know why the communist leaders consider socialism the highroad to communism.

Second, we should accept the command of the Lord and treat socialistic-communism as the tool of Satan. We should follow the counsel of the President of the Church and resist the influence and policies of the socialistic-communist conspiracy wherever they are found—in the schools, in the churches, in government, in unions, in businesses, in agriculture.

Third, we should help those who have been deceived or who are misinformed to find the truth. Unless each person who knows the truth will "stand up and speak up" it is difficult for the deceived or confused citizen to find his way back.

Fourth, we should not make the mistake of calling people "communists" just because they happen to be helping the communist cause. Thousands of patriotic Americans, including a few Latter-day Saints, have helped the communists without realizing it. Others have knowingly helped without joining the party. The remedy is to avoid name-calling, but point out clearly and persuasively how they are helping the communists.

Fifth, each priesthood holder should use his influence in the community to resist the erosion which is taking place in our political and economic life. He should use the political party of his choice to express his evaluation of important issues. He should see that his party is working to preserve freedom, not destroy it. He should join responsible local groups interested in promoting freedom and free competitive enterprise, in studying political issues, appraising the voting records and proposed programs, and writing to members of Congress, promoting good men in public office and scrutinizing local, state, and federal agencies to see that the will of the people is carried out. He should not wait for the Lord's servants to give instruction for every detail once they have announced the direction in which the priesthood should go. Each member should exercise prayerful judgment and then act.

Sixth, and most important of all, each member of the priesthood should set his own house in order. This should include:

1. Holding regular family prayer, remembering especially our government leaders.

2. Getting out of debt.

3. Seeing that each member of the family understands the importance of keeping the commandments.

4. Seeing that the truth is shared with members of the family, with neighbors, and with associates.

5. Seeing that each member is performing his duties in the priesthood, in the auxiliary organizations, in the temple, and in the civic life of the community.

6. Seeing that every wage earner in the home is a full

tithepayer and fulfilling other obligations in financial support of the kingdom.

7. Providing a one-year supply of essentials.

In doing these things a member of the Church is not only making himself an opponent of the adversary, but a *proponent* of the Lord.

In the prophecies there is no promise except to the obedient. To a modern prophet the Lord said:

"Therefore, what I say unto one, I say unto all: Watch, for the adversary spreadeth his dominions, and darkness reigneth;

"And the anger of God kindleth against the inhabitants of the earth;

". . . I give unto you directions how you may act before me, that it may turn to you for your salvation.

"I, the Lord, am bound when ye do what I say; but when ye do not what I say, ye have no promise." (D&C 82:5-6, 9-10.)

May God give us the wisdom to recognize the threat to our freedom and strength to meet this danger courageously.

(Tabernacle, Salt Lake City, Utah, October Conference, 1961.)

Be a Square

My beloved brethren and sisters, in humility and gratitude I face you this morning. I bear witness that the Book of Mormon is a sacred volume of scripture, that it is true, that it is an added witness to the divine mission of Jesus Christ, an added witness to the divinity of the Holy Bible. I bear witness that Joseph Smith is and was a Prophet of the Living God, one of the greatest, if not the greatest Prophet that ever lived upon the earth. These things I know with all my heart and thank God for this testimony.

It is an honor to participate in this wonderful program this morning. I love the MIA. Through fifty years it has touched and blessed my life, and of the many thrills that I have received and the joys that have come, I think the greatest thrill of all occurred this morning when President David O. McKay and his lovely companion surprised us by entering this meeting. This is an event, I think, that we shall never forget.

As I picked up the program for this conference in my office the other day and opened it to a full spread and looked at the cover, I received a thrill that will remain with me for many weeks and months to come. Youth looking up, looking at the world, facing the world, honestly. I thought of the father—not a very good father, I fear—who went out in the early night with his little son into a neighbor's field to steal some melons, and after looking in all directions around him he gave the signal to the son to start putting the melons into the basket. But the little six-year-old boy said, "Daddy, there's one place you didn't look."

"What's that, what's that, son? Where?"

"Daddy, you didn't look up."

We want the young people of this Church to look up, to face the world. Forty years ago while serving as a humble missionary under the inspired leadership of President David O. McKay, we had a little pamphlet entitled, "The Latter-day Saints and the World." This Church of which we are a part is a world organization. Our message is a world message. Our program is a program for the youth of the entire world. It fits anywhere. It has come forth under the inspiration of heaven, and it is being directed under that same inspiration.

You, my brethren and sisters, are called to leadership. You have been called to provide divinely inspired leadership for the youth of the Church. It is expected that you will study diligently in order to come to an understanding of the purposes, policies, and potentials of the great MIA program. Your success in the lives of people will be commensurate with your preparation, your perseverance, and your prayer-fulness. May the Spirit of the Lord always be with you.

This conference, the literature you will receive, the in-struction that will come, the notes you will take will inspire every leader to approach his assignment with confidence, enthusiasm, wisdom, and dedication. Thus, will the calling of every MIA leader be magnified to strengthen the character and increase the testimony of the youth of the Church, and may you always remember that the whole purpose of the Church is to build men and women of character, men and women of strength, men and women of faith—Godlike men and women. Character is the one thing we make in this world and take with us into the next.

"Therefore, O ye that embark in the service of God, see that ye serve him with all your heart, might, mind, and strength, that ye may stand blameless before God at the last day." (D&C 4:2.)

Think of your motto, "The Glory of God Is Intelli-gence. . . ." I sat at a luncheon given in my honor at the great Purdue University a few years ago, and at my side was the president of the university, Dr. Havde. Some twenty men were at the table. In the conversation he said, "Well, I see you Mormons have done it again." I said, "What have we done now?" He said, "You're way out in front as usual in the field of education. I have just read the annual report. How do you do it? How do you account for it? You're not a wealthy state, but you're always out in the foreground."

I said, "I'm not sure I have the answer. Maybe I can contribute a little. The Church has always placed emphasis upon education. We believe that a man is saved no faster than he gets knowledge. We believe in the great eternal principle of eternal progression, and then we have a great youth organization in the Church that we call the MIA and their theme is 'The Glory of God Is Intelligence.' "

"What is it you say?" he asked.

I repeated the theme. He said, "I never heard anything like that." Then he called the attention of these twenty men and repeated our conversation. A few moments later in the great music hall were 7,000 farmers from twelve states. As their speaker was introduced the president of this university again repeated our conversation and repeated the MIA theme, "The Glory of God Is Intelligence."

Sometimes I think we are so close to it all as MIA people we fail to appreciate the blessings of MIA.

Colors—gold and green—brought and displayed on the grounds during today's wonderful reception. Gold typifying strength, honor, and power, or the glorious heights to which youth may attain. Green denoting youth, growth, and progress.

You know the purpose of MIA—to provide a means by which the doctrines of the gospel can be more effectively taught to the young men and women, that testimonies of the truth of these doctrines and the divinity of the mission of Joseph Smth might be gained, and also that the literary tastes of the young might be developed and their social activities brought under better management and control.

You have read and will read in the new executive handbook the charge given to you as leaders by the First Presidency of the Church.

What does MIA mean? It means Mutual Improvement Association. MIA means an organization of young men and an organization of young women—two organizations working co-operatively together for mutual improvement in the spirit of unity. MIA means a helping organization—an auxiliary to the priesthood of the Church. Its purposes are to develop testimonies of the gospel, develop talents, provide social activities, provide recreational activities, develop faithful Latter-day Saints.

Yes, MIA provides spiritual growth through gospel study, spiritualized recreation through playing and praying together, cultural enrichment through social activities. MIA is for everyone twelve years of age and older.

And now, my beloved leaders, you are working with the choicest material obtainable anywhere. These young people are not just ordinary people. They are not just the run of the mill. They are choice spirits. President Wilford Woodruff said this: "The Lord has chosen a small number of choice spirits of sons and daughters out of all the creations of God, who are to inherit this earth; and this company of choice spirits have been kept in the spirit world for six thousand years to come forth in the last days to stand in the flesh in this last Dispensation of the Fulness of Times, to organize the Kingdom of God upon the earth, to build it up and to defend it . . . and to receive the eternal and everlasting Priesthood (of God)."

You cannot fail in this work. This is God's work. These are his children. This is his program. We are his helpers. If we do our part, he will not permit us to fail. Again, we live in the world, but we must not become a part of the world so far as the sins and evils of the world are concerned. Listen to the words of President David O. McKay: "Never before in the history of the Church were there so many insidious influences at work among our people as today. Never before have dangers been so threatening to our youth. There are more threatening influences enticing our boys and girls from paths of duty than there were years ago."

Yes, we're in the world. We're in a sick world, a world that is in trouble. There are strange and dangerous trends that endanger the lives and the characters and the well-being of these choice young people. Recently I read the address of Dr. Max Rafferty, Superintendent of Education of California, which has caused such a stir. May I quote a few words. He said: "Patriotism feeds upon hero-worship." You must be worthy to be heroes to these young people. They look to you. They will heed your example. They will follow your counsel if your example is right.

"Patriotism feeds upon hero-worship, and we decided to abolish heroes. . . . It is interesting and significant," says Dr. Rafferty, "that education has deliberately debunked the hero to make room for the jerk. . . . The results are plain for all to see; the worst of our youngsters growing up to become booted, side-burned, duck-tailed, unwashed, leather-jacketed slobs, whose favorite sport is ravaging little girls and stomping polio victims to death; the best of our youth coming into maturity for all the world like young people fresh from a dizzying roller-coaster ride with everything blurred, with nothing clear, with no positive standards, with everything in doubt. No wonder so many of them welsh out and squeal and turn traitor when confronted with the grim reality of a Red military force and the crafty cunning of Red psychological warfare."

Talk about need for leadership. There has never been such a great need as there is today. Your challenge is clear. These, our young people, must have a clear allegiance. They must have positive standards. They must hold to those anchors which you can provide through the program of the Church. They must be young men and women of character.

In *Scouting*, a magazine for adults, in the April issue I read an article by Charles H. Brower which has stirred me. I hope every MIA leader reads it. May I quote from it? He says: and he gives this as only one example of what is happening in the world in which we live, the world which the youth faces, how fundamentals are slipping away, how there has been a decline in the basic standards, a demoralization. And then he states this:

"Back in Mark Twain's day, 'square' was one of the finest words in our language. You gave a man a square deal if you were honest. And you gave him a square meal when he was hungry. When you got out of debt you were square with the world. And that was when you could look your fellow man squarely in the eye.

"Then a lot of strange characters got hold of this honest, wholesome word, bent it all out of shape, and gave it back to our children. Now everyone knows what a square is. He's the man who never learned to get away with it. A Joe who volunteers when he doesn't have to. A guy who gets his kicks from trying to do something better than anyone else. A boob who gets so lost in his work that he has to be reminded to go home. A slob who still gets all choked up when he hears 'America the Beautiful.' "

We want to rear young men and women to be squares if this is what squares are. Young men and women who can get choked up when they hear "America the Beautiful!" Going on, this author says, "His tribe, the square, isn't thriving too well. He doesn't fit into the current group of angle players, corner cutters, sharpshooters, and goofoffs. He doesn't want to fly now and pay later. He's burdened down with old-fashioned ideas of honesty, loyalty, courage, and thrift. He may already be on his way to extinction. He and all the rest of us live in a country quite different from the one we were taught to love. Conformity is sweeping the country. While more and more people want to get seats in the grandstand, fewer and fewer want to sweat it out down on the field."

Leaders of youth, we want our young people on the field. We want them sweating it out. We want them to have responsibility, because they grow under responsibility. We are not a Church of organized sitters. We are a Church of organized workers, and we want our young people to get into it, with all their enthusiasm and power. Further on in the article Brower says, "It is easy to prove that Nathan Hale, Patrick Henry, Paul Revere, George Washington, Benjamin Franklin, and almost every one else you care to include among our national heroes was a square. Think what they might have said had they not been squares.

"*Nathan Hale:* Me spy on the British! Are you kidding? Do you know what they do with spies they catch? I'll give you a flash, chum, they hang them.

"*Paul Revere:* What do you mean, ride through every Middlesex village? And in the middle of the night yet. Why me? Am I the only man in Boston who has a horse?

"*Patrick Henry:* Sure I'm for liberty—first, last and always. But we've got to be a little realistic. We're a pretty small outfit. If we start pushing the British around someone is going to get hurt.

"*George Washington:* Gentlemen, I am honored. But try someone else—say General Gates. I'm just getting things organized at Mount Vernon. Also you might say I already served my time. Against the French, you know.

"*Benjamin Franklin:* What we really need as Ambassador to France is a young man. I'm 70 years old. It's time a new generation took over."

Well, that's not so funny. Perhaps it is significant that such men, such patriots, that what they actually did say has been quietly sneaked out of the schoolbooks of today.

Is that a challenge for the leaders of youth in this Church? *This Week Magazine* recently surveyed history books issued before 1920 and compared them with those being used today, issued since 1920.

Nathan Hale said, "I regret that I have but one life to give for my country," in eleven of the old textbooks, but in only one of the new textbooks. *Patrick Henry* said, "Give me liberty or give me death" in twelve out of the fourteen earlier texts, but in only two out of the forty-five recent texts. But *John Paul Jones* set the record. He said, "I have not yet begun to fight," in nine of the old books and in none of the new books.

Is this a challenge? Today's world! Today's world is warped. We must give direction to our young people. When Dwight D. Eisenhower was President, he appointed a Committee on National Goals to decide where we were going. Perhaps a first step should be a commission on National Heritage to make sure we remember where we have been.

May I remind you that of the twenty-one notable civilizations that have existed, of which we have record, nineteen of them perished, not from external conquest, but from the evaporation of belief within. Today, our country still has a choice. I believe it has already begun to make that choice. Gatherings such as this give me hope. I believe it is going back to its old beliefs in such things as ideas, pride, patriotism, loyalty, devotion, and even hard work and faith in God.

Yes, the struggle is on, and it's very real. Our great leader sees it clearly. Let me quote further his words. "Some of our boys and girls think the standards of morality have changed," said President McKay. "The standard of morality of the Latter-day Saint boy and girl will never change. Standards of the outside may change, may be lowered, and that influence may penetrate our social organization, but our standards must be maintained. Our boys and girls must know these standards. On whom rests this responsibility? The MIA with its classwork and with its activities of music, dance, sports, and drama—all tend to make for our young people (and for those who like to stay young) a very complete and desirable way of life."

Yes, I think there are indications that there is being a slow reversal to these basic fundamental concepts. Twenty years ago half of us belonged to churches, but today sixty-four percent of us belong. I realize that some churches have watered down their beliefs in the divine mission of Jesus Christ. They no longer accept him as the Redeemer of the world and the Savior of mankind, but it is heartening to know that sixty-four percent of our people are affiliated. There are fifty percent more symphony orchestras today than there were ten years ago. Expenditures for all cultural activities have increased seventy percent in the past ten years. Since the turn of the century, the percentage of our population that has graduated from high school is up ten times, and the percentage that has gone to college is up seven times.

But the greatest thing that has happened is that our nation has a whole new set of heroes. Their names are Cooper, Glenn, Shepard, and others. These lads grew up to be squares, for who but a square would volunteer his life for his country? They are not even ashamed of their feelings. John Glenn says he gets a funny feeling down inside when he sees the flag go by.

Can you inspire that same feeling in the youth whom you direct? Imagine that. He's proud of his small town, proud of his small college, proud that he is associated with scouting. I wish you could have seen Cooper come onto the stand at the annual meeting of the Boy Scouts in New York City last month, surrounded by hundreds and thousands of leaders of boys. Then to have them bring onto the platform, as a surprise, Cooper's Scoutmaster of years ago, and to see those two men throw their arms around each other as they thought back to the days of that Scout troop.

Mr. Brower suggests that we all join the SOS—the Society of Squares.

Some three or four years ago I had the honor of addressing the National Youthpower Congress of young rural boys and girls in a great auditorium in Chicago. It was a thrilling experience. Only the other day I received from my good friend, Charles B. Shuman, head of our greatest farm organization, his feelings after facing this group of young men at another National Youthpower Congress, and he said, "Despite the 'twist,' far-out slang and hot rod cars, today's teenagers are America's greatest national resource—our best hope for the future. They are energetic, imaginative, enthusiastic, capable, and optimistic—they have what it takes to straighten out the mess that the present generation has made of things, provided we give them half a chance. And what a mess it is—suspicion and hatred in a world divided into two armed camps, a three-hundred-billion dollar national debt for future generations to pay; widespread unemployment and inflation; and a prevailing attitude of irresponsibility. Facing these and other problems, it would not be surprising if our youngsters turned into a 'beat' generation, but fortunately, they show no signs of discouragement. . . ."

I think that spirit is in the Church among our young people. "It is never too late to change direction. Let us make a start," said this good man, "and give these, the finest young people ever produced, a chance to use their Youthpower. They may be able to lift us from the mess we have made."

I have faith in them, these our sons and daughters. They will respond to good leadership. They are entitled to good leadership. Another hopeful sign—I saw a full-page editorial in a great farm magazine the other day by the publisher and editor addressed to the graduates, from the most widely quoted farm writer in America. He was talking to these young people, not a member of the Church, but a man who is looking to the future and wants them to go right, wants them to get back, to become squares again. He says, "A person who aims at nothing has a target he can't miss. Set an attainable goal. When you reach it, set another goal, higher. Many people flounder on the ship of life because they never chart a course. Make money the by-product, not the goal. Drink at the fountain of knowledge, don't just gargle. . . ."

And then he talks about homemaking and preparation for motherhood, if you would, in a farm magazine. This is encouraging. Then he uses that old Southern phrase. He said, "Kissin' don't last but good cookin' do." And then he goes on to say, "Don't ever let anybody sell you the idea that chastity is out of date. Chastity will never be out of date. Your children will want their mother to be as pure as you want your mother to be."

Does that sound like Mormonism? Of course it does. Truth always sounds the same. It's always consistent, no matter where it comes from, and time is always on the side of truth. Going on with his interesting editorial he says, "If we lose our morality we will be enslaved, . . . Freedom and morality are one ball of wax. . . . Remember, freedom, while God-given, does not perpetuate itself. Government can give you nothing but what it takes from somebody else. A government big enough to give you everything you want is big enough to take everything you've got, including your freedom. . . . You should be rewarded according to your ability and your effort, not your needs. . . . If you're determined to milk all possible pleasure out of life, then buy your own milk, don't milk somebody else's through the fence. . . . Stand on your own feet. Every person can excel in something," he says, and then goes on, "In the final analysis, neither your government nor your parents are responsible for you—you are responsible for yourself. Believe in your God, in your country, and in yourself, and in that order. Repeat constantly to yourself: 'It all depends on me.' "

And then he said what I have heard our beloved leader of this Church say time and time again, "You can't help it if you're ugly at eighteen, but if you're not beautiful at eighty, it's your own fault." And before us today we have an example, at ninety. [President and Sister McKay] Nothing could be lovelier, more beautiful, more impressive. "Character is a victory, not a gift."

Confucius said: "To know what is right and not do it is the worst of cowardice." Yes, there will be trials and disappointments to our young people, but I am convinced that any person who has real faith in God and a testimony of this work can endure anything and still keep his spirit sweet. We want our young people prepared so they can endure anything. Whatever comes, they can meet it without being concerned a lot about it, without breaking up, without being frustrated, knowing that they and God above, calling on our heritage of the past, will carry them through.

Today we have an opportunity the like of which we have never had in the Church. All over the world the Church is well spoken of. Today we are known for what we are and not for what our enemies have said about us in the past. What an opportunity to "arise and shine forth" as the Lord has commanded. Read it in the one hundred and fifteenth section of the Doctrine and Covenants and the eighty-third section. Now is the time to wield our influence for good in this world which is sick. Now is the time for us as leaders of youth to prepare these young men and women for the difficult days ahead.

How are we going to do it? First of all, we must look to ourselves. We must be what we profess to be, real Latter-day Saints—not Jack-Mormons. We must maintain every standard of this Church. We must keep the command-

ments. We must set our own lives in order. We must set
our homes in order. We must be modest. We must be
humble. We must be clean, morally clean—clean in our
own hearts and in our own minds. We must be what we
want our followers to be. We cannot be effective, if while
we teach them the Word of Wisdom, we are serving tea and
coffee and cocktails in our homes.

We cannot be effective if we are going out to card parties when we ought to be home reading the scriptures, tending our families, or spending more time with the youth of the
Church. We cannot be effective if we neglect our family
prayer. We cannot be effective if we are not honorable in
our dealings with our fellow men. We cannot be effective
if we let down in our standards.

Let's be what we want them to be. They need fewer
critics and more models. They are entitled to that kind of
leadership. What will we teach them? May I say in conclusion there are so many things to teach them. The whole
program of the Church, all the principles of the gospel, all
of the standards, the ideals, the traditions, the heritage. No
group of young people has so much to draw upon if they
only have the leaders that will draw it and feed it to them.

President McKay said the other day, "Never has the
enemy of righteousness been more thoroughly organized
than today." The world is walking in darkness, spiritual
darkness at noonday. Let us keep our eyes on the Prophet.
Let us teach these young people to keep their eyes on the
Prophet of the Lord, to pray for him, to be loyal to him,
to read his words, to heed his counsel. Let us have them
believe and know that it pays to live the good life. Let us
have them know that Jesus is the Christ, the Redeemer of
the world, our Advocate with the Father, our great exemplar.

Let us teach them to love the prophets who have served
as mouthpieces for God Almighty. Let us teach them a
love for the pioneers. Teach them to be proud of their
heritage, grateful for their foundations, for all the virtues and
principles for which the Church stands.

Teach them to love their country, and here in America to love the Constitution and the founding fathers, and to know that this is the Lord's base of operations in these last days, and that that operation will be world-wide. Teach them that this system that offers so many of the good things of life is based on eternal principles, the great principle of free agency.

Teach them to love purity and virtue and the good life. Teach them to love all the commandments, and that they are given to them for their good by a kind Father who loves them. Teach them to love life, to love the Church and its programs, and to get in the full swing of it.

Teach them to love the scriptures, to love the Book of Mormon. The Prophet Joseph Smith declared ". . . that the Book of Mormon was the most correct of any book on earth, and the keystone of our religion, and a man would get nearer to God by abiding by its precepts, than by any other book." (*DHC* 4, p. 461.) Teach them to become a companion to the Book of Mormon.

Teach them to know that God has again spoken from the heavens, that that first great vision is the greatest event that has transpired in this world since the resurrection of the Master.

God bless you, my fellow workers in this great program of MIA. May you be magnified. May you have the Spirit, without which you cannot teach effectively. Again I say, in this work you cannot fail. This is God's work. I know this as I know that I live. God help us to keep that knowledge and to inspire that testimony in the lives of these choice young people under our custody, I pray in the name of Jesus Christ. Amen.

(*Tabernacle, MIA June Conference*, June 14, 1963.)

A World Message

I stand before you this morning in deep humility and gratitude, my brothers and sisters, rejoicing in the opportunities and blessings which have been mine to be in attendance at this conference. With all my heart I endorse the counsel that has been given and add my witness to those testimonies already borne.

I think it was Edgar A. Guest who said:

> Some folks leave home for money
>   And some leave home for fame,
> Some seek skies always sunny,
>   And some depart in shame.
> I care not what the reason
>   Men travel east or west,
> Or what the time or season—
>   The home-town is the best.

I am so happy, my brethren and sisters, to be with you today back here in the bosom of the Church, and to realize that I can probably remain here beyond the end of this conference session this afternoon.

As I drove west a few days ago from my home of eight years in Washington to these valleys of the mountains, I caught myself singing many of the old familiar Mormon hymns: "O Ye Mountains High," "Beautiful Zion for Me." I had a great joy in my heart, and I had a great surge of freedom, I think augmented somewhat by the fact that I was behind the wheel of my own car after riding behind government chauffeurs for eight years.

It is good to be home. There is one expression that has become very dear to me. It has been repeated over and over again, I guess, hundreds of times by many people during the last few days: "Brother Benson, it is good to have you home again." It isn't half so good to have me home as it is for me to be home. It is a joy, my brethren and sisters, to be here to enjoy the warm welcome and the sweet spirit of brotherhood and fellowship that we have in the Church. I know it is very real. Of course, it isn't what it should be. It isn't what it could be. It isn't what it will be, as we continue to increase our faith and live more fully the gospel of Jesus Christ. But it is truly a sweet spirit.

I am grateful for the privilege of being back again associating with my brethren of the General Authorities. There is no sweeter association in all this world among men than the association we enjoy as a body of General Authorities of the Church. And I say this after having traveled almost a million miles in forty-five nations during the last eight years. And I am grateful to be a part of this brotherhood, this fellowship, this spirit, which is part of the Church and kingdom of God.

I express my gratitude this morning for the interest that has been shown in my activities during recent years, for the support that has been given to my humble efforts. These have been eight rather difficult, eventful, and I must say, rewarding years. I have had a prayer in my heart constantly that I would never do anything that would hurt the Church, or my great country—your country.

I have missed the association of the brethren of the General Authorities. I think the happiest hour each week has been on Sunday when I had the pleasure of reading the minutes of the weekly meeting of the First Presidency and the Council of the Twelve, held in the upper room of the Salt Lake Temple. I am grateful to President McKay for kindly granting me this privilege.

I have missed the weekly travels to the stakes and mission of the Church, and yet I have had the glorious privilege of meeting the Saints in many parts of the world. I have had a conviction, through all this period, my brethren and sisters, that I was where the Lord wanted me to be. I hope and pray that I will always be where he wants me to be. I have had no doubt of that since President McKay in November 1952, realizing that there might be a request for me to occupy an important government position, said to me: "Brother Benson, my mind is clear, and if the opportunity comes in the proper spirit, I think you should accept."

The opportunity came in the proper spirit on a high spiritual plane, and I accepted. We have a responsibility as American citizens to respond to the calls of Presidents of the United States. As a humble stake president I had responded to such a call from President Franklin Delano Roosevelt and served for some time on a four-man national agricultural advisory committee during the 1940's.

But the thing I am most grateful for this morning is the faith and prayers that have been exercised in my behalf during the last eight years—first of all by my brethren of the General Authorities, by the members of my own quorum, by the First Presidency and others, by my devoted family, and my companion who always has come to the rescue especially during crucial periods—and we have had a few. I shall ever be grateful for the faith and prayers of the Latter-day Saints throughout the Church and for the faith and prayers of the people of all faiths from all over the free world. Hundreds, yes, thousands of letters, telegrams, telephone calls, and other messages have given ample evidence of the great amount of faith and prayer that has been exercised in my behalf. Without this faith and without this help I am sure I could not possibly have accomplished even the small amount that I have been able to do.

Yes, it has been a politically sensitive position. There have been honest differences. Thank God we live in a land where men and women can differ honestly without fear. I have been in countries where that is not possible. I know that some of the differences have probably been inspired by political expediency, but on the whole I think they have been honest differences.

There has been criticism, too, but I am frank and honest in saying that it has never bothered me very much, because in my heart I have been convinced I was doing the thing that seemed to me, at least, to be right, and the thing which our mail and other evidence also indicated represented the views of the overwhelming majority of the American people. And I have nothing in my heart, nor have I had, except a love for the people. I have had no bitterness. I have no bitterness today. At times when the wonderful representatives of the press, who have been such a help, have said, "Surely, you must hate these people who criticize you," I have usually replied, "I do not hate any living soul. I love all of our Father's children. True, I love some more than others."

But honestly, my brethren and sisters, I have had no feeling of bitterness or hatred in my heart, for which I am deeply grateful because I have prayed—we have prayed as a family—that we could avoid any spirit of hatred or bitterness. I love our Father's children. I think the great rank and file of them are good. Oh, they have weaknesses—all of us do—but as I have visited them in forty-five nations, I found that they are very much the same. True, some of them have bad leaders. Some of them have lost that which is priceless, yea, even more priceless than life itself—their freedom, their right to choose, their right to make their own decisions. But on the whole they are good people.

I like to think they have five things in common—five aspirations, five hopes. I have found that universally they long for peace, and I am confident that if the leaders of this world or of the nations of the earth respond to the will of the people, they will work and labor and pray for peace.

Secondly, they want to live as brothers, as neighbors, and friends. Third, they love their homes and families, and on the whole they want to be good parents. Fourth, they want to raise their standards of living. They want to enjoy some of the comforts of life, some of the opportunities for development and growth and culture. And fifth, they desire to do good.

Now, most of these people have been from the rural areas, but keep in mind that the rural people of this world represent more than half of the total population. They are people who have had their feet in the soil, who have been close to the land, who live and work in the country, and they are solid, substantial people, not easily stampeded, who probably know about as well as any other segment of our population that "as ye sow, so shall ye reap."

I am grateful for the people I have worked with. I am grateful that my lot has been cast in large measure with the rural people of the world. I am grateful for the support I have had from many of these wonderful people, from the wonderful group of men who have been associated with me in the Department of Agriculture, for their spirit of loyalty and unity and devoted service. I am very grateful for the support I have had from the Chief Executive during these eight years, for his loyalty, for his deep spirituality, for his determination to do that which he believed to be right and to approve my doing so as well. Also I am grateful that he remained true to his promise that I would never be asked to support any program or policy which I did not believe in, and I am sure he knew in his own heart that I would not do it anyway.

I say I love our Father's children. Hundreds and thousands of them I have contacted during the last eight years. Last night in the priesthood meeting we heard about the great "share the gospel" program and the referral program. I have the names of some 9,000 men, approximately, with whom I have had personal contact in an official capacity. I hope to give referral cards for them. I would like to have every one of them hear the gospel. I wish that all of our Father's children might enjoy the blessings that come through an acceptance and living of the gospel of Jesus Christ.

Yes, even when I was in Russia, I expressed the hope to the Russian leaders, our hosts, that after my tour of duty was over for the government that I might have the opportunity of returning to Russia and being privileged to hold meetings to discuss my philosophy of life and to talk about things spiritual with the wonderful Russian people. Of course, I was not given a promise. The leaders of communism are afraid of the light of truth. But it is my hope and prayer, my brethren and sisters, that some time in some way the door may be opened in all the nations of the earth, that they might receive the message of the restored gospel; that they might enjoy the blessings of freedom under a system similar to what we enjoy here in this great land—a system that has brought us so much joy and happiness and so many of the good things of life—a system based on freedom of choice, on the private ownership of property, on the right to exchange our goods and services with our neighbors.

Yes, I love this great land. It has been an honor to serve. I know that this nation has a prophetic history. I would to God that every citizen of this land might read the Book of Mormon prayerfully and learn something of the prophecies made regarding this land—the promises made and the conditions upon which they are made—that we might as an American people so live that these great promises could be fully realized; that we might come to know that the Constitution of this land has been established by men whom the God of heaven raised up unto that very purpose.

This nation has a great mission to perform. Here was prepared the place where the gospel could be restored as has been told so beautifully by Brother Tanner. It is my conviction that the world needs, as it needs no other thing, the gospel of Jesus Christ, and the people of the world want what the gospel will give, but they do not realize it. They want the anchor which the gospel provides, which gives them the answers to the problems that face them; that brings them a feeling of security and a feeling of inner peace. The gospel is the only answer to the problems of the world, my brethren and sisters. We may cry peace. We may hold peace conferences. And I have nothing but commendation for those who work for peace. But it is my conviction that peace must come from within. It cannot be imposed by state mandate. It can come only by following the teachings and the example of the Prince of Peace.

Yes, I am happy to be back home. It is my hope and prayer that I may be able to help in some small way to carry this glorious message to our Father's children. I have hoped and prayed that my services in the last eight years may have contributed somewhat to the great missionary effort of the Church. I wish that we might go to all the world—to Israel, where I have had the opportunity of two extensive visits recently, where miracles are being performed, where prophecies are being fulfilled. I wish we could go to the wonderful Arab countries. I shall never forget how I was received with open arms, how the hand of friendship and fellowship was extended to me there.

I shall never forget my visit to Egypt, and as a tangible evidence further of their love and friendship, they offered to me one of their choicest prized gifts—a wonderful Arabian stallion. I would like to see us carry the gospel to India, to the humble people of that land; to Pakistan, to China, to Yugoslavia, to Poland, to Russia, everywhere, because, my brethren and sisters, our message is a world message. This Church is a world organization.

A hundred and thirty years ago, when the elders were assembled in conference to determine whether the revelations should be published to the world, the Lord saw fit to give a revelation to his Church, which was also directed to the world. He referred to it as his "Preface," or his "Introduction to his Book of Commandments," and it is the first section of the Doctrine and Covenants, from which I quote these words: (Note them carefully.)

"Hearken, O ye people of my church, saith the voice of him who dwells on high, and whose eyes are upon all men; yea, verily I say: Hearken ye people from afar; and ye that are upon the islands of the sea, listen together.

"For verily the voice of the Lord is unto all men, and there is none to escape; . . .

"And the voice of warning shall be unto all people, by the mouths of my disciples, whom I have chosen in these last days.

"And they shall go forth and none shall stay them, for I the Lord have commanded them." (D&C 1:1-2, 4-5.)

So our message is a world message. It is intended for all of our Father's children. When God the Father and his Son Jesus Christ saw fit to come here to earth and appear to a boy prophet, surely such a visitation was intended to bless all of our Father's children.

I testify to you today, my brethren and sisters, that the gospel is true; that it has been restored to the earth in its purity, in its fulness. Mormonism is the gospel of Jesus Christ in its fulness, and therefore Mormonism is true. God help us to live the gospel. I testify to you that God has again spoken from the heavens. The heavens are not sealed. The vision of God the Father and the Son to the boy prophet did in very deed occur. God lives. Jesus is the Christ, the Redeemer of the world, not just a great moral teacher, as much of the Christian world is claiming, but the Savior of mankind, the very Son of God.

Joseph Smith was a Prophet of the Living God, one of the greatest prophets that has ever lived upon the earth. He was the instrument in God's hand in ushering in a great gospel dispensation, the greatest ever, and the last of all in preparation for the second coming of the Master.

I bear witness that these things are true, and that we have standing at the head of the Church today a prophet of the Living God, who holds all the keys and authority necessary to carry forward our Father's program for the blessing of his children. As God lives, I know these things to be true and bear this witness to you, my brethren and sisters, in the name of the Lord Jesus Christ. Amen.

(Tabernacle, Salt Lake City, Utah, April Conference 1961.)

Be Not Deceived

Humbly and gratefully I approach you today. Humble in the awesome task of speaking to you—grateful for the gospel, and a prophet at our head! I concur in this great address on man and free agency given by the Lord's mouthpiece. President McKay will go down in eternity as one of the great champions of free men.

Years ago my great-grandfather, while an investigator, attended a Mormon meeting during which a member had a quarrel over the Sacrament table with the branch president. When the service was over, Mrs. Benson turned to Ezra T. and asked him what he thought of the Mormons now. I'll always be grateful for his answer. He said he thought the actions of its members in no way altered the truth of Mormonism. That conviction saved him from many a tragedy. Before joining the Church, Grandfather was moved by a marvelous prayer of Apostle John E. Page.

But later the young convert was greatly shocked by the same man whose actions reflected his gradual apostasy.

Ironically, when Elder Page eventually was excommunicated, Brigham Young selected the young convert to fill his place in the Quorum of the Twelve.

Six of the original Twelve Apostles selected by Joseph Smith were excommunicated. The Three Witnesses to the Book of Mormon left the Church. Three of Joseph Smith's Counselors fell—one even helped plot his death.

A natural question that might arise would be, that if the Lord knew in advance that these men would fall, as he undoubtedly did, why did he have his prophet call them to such high office? The answer is: to fill the Lord's purposes. For even the Master followed the will of the Father by selecting Judas. President George Q. Cannon suggests an explanation, too, when he states:

"Perhaps it is His own design that faults and weaknesses should appear in high places in order that His Saints may learn to trust in Him and not in any man or men." (*Millennial Star*, 53:658-659. February 15, 1891.)

And this would parallel Nephi's warning; put not your "trust in the arm of flesh." (2 Nephi 4:34.)

"The Church," says President McKay, "is little, if at all, injured by persecution and calumnies from ignorant, misinformed, or malicious enemies." (*The Instructor*, February, 1956, p. 33.)

It is from within the Church that the greatest hindrance comes. And so, it seems, it has been. Now the question arises, will we stick with the kingdom and can we avoid being deceived? Certainly this is an important question, for the Lord has said that in the last days the "devil will rage in the hearts of men" (2 Nephi 28:20), and if it were possible "he shall deceive the very elect." (See Writings of Joseph Smith 2:5-37.)

"The adversary," said BrighamYoung, "presents his principles and arguments in the most approved style, and in the most winning tone, attended with the most graceful attitudes; and he is very careful to ingratiate himself into the favor of the powerful and influential of mankind, uniting himself with popular parties, floating into offices of trust and emolument by pandering to popular feeling, though it should seriously wrong and oppress the innocent. Such characters put on the manners of an angel, appearing as nigh like angels of light as they possibly can, to deceive the innocent and the unwary. The good which they do, they do it to bring to pass an evil purpose upon the good and honest followers of Jesus Christ." (*JD* 11, pp. 238-239.)

Those of us who think "all is well in Zion" (2 Nephi 28:21), in spite of Book of Mormon warning, might ponder the words of Heber C. Kimball when he said, "Yes, we think we are secure here in the chambers of these everlasting hills . . . but I want to say to you, my brethren, the time is coming when we will be mixed up in these now peaceful valleys to that extent that it will be difficult to tell the face of a Saint from the face of an enemy against the people of God. Then is the time to look out for the great sieve, for there will be a great sifting time, and many will fall. For I say unto you there is a test, a Test, a TEST coming." (Heber C. Kimball, 1856. Quoted by J. Golden Kimball, *Conference Report*, October 1930, pp. 59, 60.)

One of the greatest discourses that I have ever heard or read on how to avoid being deceived was given from this pulpit during the priesthood session of the October, 1960 semiannual conference by Elder Marion G. Romney. (*Conference Report*, October 1960, p. 73.) I commend it to you for your close study, and wish that there were time to re-read it. During the talk Elder Romney stated that there was no guarantee that the devil will not deceive a lot of men who hold the priesthood. Then, after referring to a talk on free agency by President McKay, Elder Romney states, "Free agency is the principle against which Satan waged his war in heaven. It is still the front on which he makes his most furious, devious, and persistent attacks. That this would be the case was foreshadowed by the Lord."

And then after quoting the scripture from the Pearl of Great Price regarding the war in heaven over free agency (Moses 4:1-4) Elder Romney continues:

"You see, at the time he was cast out of heaven, his objective was (and still is) 'to deceive and to blind men, and to lead them captive at his will.' This he effectively does to as many as will not hearken unto the voice of God. His main attack is still on free agency. When he can get men to yield their agency, he has them well on the way to captivity.

"We who hold the priesthood must beware concerning

ourselves, that we do not fall into the traps he lays to rob us of our freedom. We must be careful that we are not led to accept or support in any way any organization, cause or measure which, in its remotest effect, would jeopardize free agency, whether it be in politics, government, religion, employment, education, or in any other field. It is not enough for us to be sincere in what we support. We must be right!"

Elder Romney then outlined some tests to distinguish the true from the counterfeit. Now this is crucial for us to know, for as President Taylor said, "Besides the preaching of the gospel, we have another mission, namely, the perpetuation of the free agency of man and the maintenance of liberty, freedom and the rights of man." (*JD* 23, p. 63.)

It was the struggle over free agency that divided us before we came here; it may well be the struggle over the same principle which will deceive and divide us again.

May I suggest three short tests to avoid being deceived, both pertaining to this freedom struggle and all other matters

1. What do the standard works have to say about it? "To the law and to the testimony: If they speak not according to this word, it is because there is no light in them" said Isaiah. (Isaiah 8:20.) (2 Nephi 18:20.) And Hosea said, "My people are destroyed for lack of knowledge. . . ." (Hosea 4:6.)

We must diligently study the scriptures. Of special importance to us are the Book of Mormon and the Doctrine and Covenants. Joseph Smith said, ". . . that the Book of Mormon was the most correct of any book on earth, and the keystone of our religion, and a man would get nearer to God by abiding by its precepts, than by any other book." (*History of the Church*, Vol. 1, p. 461.)

The Book of Mormon, Brigham Young said, was written on the tablets of his heart and no doubt helped save him from being deceived. The Book of Mormon has a lot to say about America, freedom and secret combinations.

The Doctrine and Covenants is important because it contains the revelations which helped lay the foundation of this great latter-day work. It speaks of many things. In section 134 (verse 2) it states that government should hold inviolate the right and control of property. This makes important reading in a day when government controls are increasing and people are losing the right to control their own property.

The second guide is; what do the latter-day Presidents of the Church have to say on the subject—particularly the living President? President Wilford Woodruff related an instant in church history when Brigham Young was addressing a congregation in the presence of the Prophet Joseph Smith;

"Brother Brigham took the stand, and he took the Bible and laid it down; he took the Book of Mormon, and laid it down; and he took the Book of Doctrine and Covenants, and laid it down before him, and he said; 'There is the written word of God to us, concerning the work of God from the beginning of the world, almost, to our day. And now,' said he, 'when compared with the living oracles, those books are nothing to me; those books do not convey the word of God direct to us now, as do the words of a Prophet or a man bearing the Holy Priesthood in our day and generation. I would rather have the living oracles than all the writing in the books.' That was the course he pursued. When he was through, Brother Joseph said to the congregation; 'Brother Brigham has told you the word of the Lord, and he has told you the truth.' . . ." (*Conference Report*, October 1897, pp. 18-19.)

There is only one man on the earth today who speaks for the Church. (D&C 132:7; 21:4.) That man is President

David O. McKay. Because he gives the word of the Lord
for us today his words have an even more immediate importance than those of the dead prophets. When speaking
under the influence of the Holy Ghost his words are scripture. (D&C 68:4.) I commend for your reading the masterful discourse of President J. Reuben Clark in the *Church
News* of July 31, 1954, entitled: "When Are Church Leader's
Words Entitled to Claim of Scripture?"

The President can speak on any subject he feels is
needful for the Saints. As Brigham Young has stated: "I
defy any man on earth to point out the path a Prophet of
God should walk in, or point out his duty, and just how
far he must go, in dictating temporal or spiritual things.
Temporal and spiritual things are inseparably connected,
and ever will be." (*JD* 10:364.) Other officers in the kingdom have fallen but never the Presidents. Keep your
eye on the Captain is still good counsel. The words of a
living prophet must and ever will take precedence.

President McKay has said a lot about our tragic trends
towards socialism and communism and the responsibilities
liberty-loving people have in defending and preserving our
Constitution. (See *Conference Report,* April 1963, pp. 112-
113.) Have we read these words from God's mouthpiece
and pondered on them?

The third and final test is the Holy Ghost—the test of
the spirit. By the spirit we "may know the truth of all
things." (Moroni 10:5.) This test can only be fully effective if one's channels of communication with God are clean
and virtuous and uncluttered with sin. Said Brigham
Young:

"You may know whether you are led right or wrong;
as well as you know the way home; for every principle God
has revealed carries its own convictions of its truth to the
human mind. . . . What a pity it would be if we were led
by one man to utter destruction! Are you afraid of this?

I am more afraid that this people have so much confidence in their leaders that they will not inquire of themselves of God whether they are led by Him. I am fearful they settle down in a state of blind self-security, trusting their eternal destiny in the hands of their leaders with a reckless confidence that in itself would thwart the purposes of God in their salvation, and weaken that influence they could give to their leaders, did they know for themselves, by the revelations of Jesus, that they are led in the right way. Let every man and women know, by the whispering of the Spirit of God to themselves, whether their leaders are walking in the path the Lord dictates or not. This has been my exhortation continually." (*JD* 9:149-150.)

Elder Heber C. Kimball stated: "The time will come when no man or woman will be able to endure on borrowed light." (*Idem.*)

How then can we know whether a man is speaking by the spirit? The Bible, Book of Mormon, and Doctrine and Covenants give us the key. (D&C 50:17-23; 100:5-8; 2 Nephi 33:1; 1 Cor. 2:10-11.) President Clark summarized them well when he said:

"We can tell when the speakers are moved upon by the Holy Ghost only when we, ourselves, are moved upon by the Holy Ghost. In a way, this completely shifts the responsibility from them to us to determine when they so speak . . . the Church will know by the testimony of the Holy Ghost in the body of the members, whether the brethren in voicing their views are moved upon by the Holy Ghost; and in due time that knowledge will be made manifest." (*Deseret News, Church Section* July 31, 1954.)

Will this Spirit be needed to check actions in other situations? Yes, and it could be used as a guide and a protector for the faithful in a situation described by Elder Lee at the last general priesthood session of the Church when he said:

"In the history of the Church there have been times or instances where Counselors in the First Presidency and others in high station have sought to overturn the decision or to persuade the President contrary to his inspired judgment, and always, if you will read carefully the history of the Church, such oppositions brought not only disastrous results to those who resisted the decision of the President, but almost always such temporary persuasions were called back for reconsideration, or a reversal of hasty action not in accordance with the feelings, the inspired feelings, of the President of the Church. And that, I submit, is one of the fundamental things that we must never lose sight of in the building of the kingdom of God." (*Conference Report,* April 1963, p. 81.)

These then, are the three tests: The standard works; the inspired words of the Presidents of the Church, particularly the living President; and the promptings of the Holy Ghost.

Now, brothers and sisters, in this great struggle for free agency just think what a power for good we could be in this world if we were united. Remember how President Clark used to reiterate in the general priesthood meeting of the Church that there was not a righteous thing in this world that we couldn't accomplish if we were only united.

And President McKay has reiterated it again and again when he's stated: "Next to being one in worshiping God, there is nothing in this world upon which this Church should be more united than in upholding and defending the Constitution of the United States!

"May the appeal of our Lord in his intercessory prayer for unity be realized in our homes, our wards, our stakes, and in our support of the basic principles of our Republic," said President McKay. (*The Instructor,* February 1956, p. 34.)

To that I say Amen and Amen!

President McKay speaks of a unity on principles. President Clark said:

"God provided that in this land of liberty, our political allegiance shall run not to individuals, that is, to government officials, no matter how great or how small they may be. Under his plan our allegiance and the only allegiance we owe as citizens or denizens of the United States, runs to our inspired Constitution which God himself set up. So runs the oath of office of those who participate in government. A certain loyalty we do owe to the office which a man holds, but even here we owe, just by reason of our citizenship, no loyalty to the man himself. In other countries it is to the individual that allegiance runs. This principle of allegiance to the Constitution is basic to our freedom. It is one of the great principles that distinguishes this 'land of liberty' from other countries.

"Thus God added to his priceless blessings to us.

"I wish to say with all the earnestness I possess that when you youth and maidens see any curtailment of these liberties I have named, when you see government invading any of these realms of freedom which we have under our Constitution, you will know that they are putting shackles on your liberty, and that tyranny is creeping upon you, no matter who curtails these liberties or who invades these realms, and no matter what the reason and excuse therefor may be." (*The Improvement Era*, July 1940, p. 444.)

We all should know by now what President McKay has said about liberty-loving peoples' greatest responsibility. We've heard him tell of our drift toward socialism and communism. We know of his feelings regarding recent tragic decisions of the Supreme Court. We know the church position supporting right to work laws and the church opposition to programs of federal aid to education. These and many more things has President McKay told us that involve this great struggle against state slavery and the anti-Christ. Now, inasmuch as all these warnings have come through the only mouthpiece of the Lord on the earth today there is one major question we should ask ourselves. Assuming we are living a life so we can know, then what does the Holy Spirit have to say about it?

We are under obligation to answer this question. God will hold us responsible.

Let us not be deceived in the sifting days ahead. Let us rally together on principle behind the prophet as guided by the promptings of the Spirit.

We should continue to speak out for freedom and against socialism and communism as President McKay has consistently admonished us. We should continue to come to the aid of patriots, programs, and organizations which are trying to save our Constitution through every legal and moral means possible.

God has not left us in darkness regarding these matters. We have the scriptures—ancient and modern. We have a living prophet, and we may obtain the Spirit.

Joseph Smith did see the Father and the Son. The kingdom established through the Prophet's instrumentality will roll forth.

We can move forward with it.

That we may all do so and be not deceived is my humble prayer.

(*Tabernacle, Salt Lake City, Utah, October Conference, 1963.*)

Index

More reading from Archive Publishers:

November 23, 2016

More reading from Archive Publishers:

FAITH-PROMOTING SERIES

Faith Promoting Series (Complete 17 book set)	149.95
Early Scenes in Church History (George C. Lambert)	8.95
Eventful Narratives (Juvenile Instructor Office)	7.95
Fragments of Experience (Juvenile Instructor Office)	9.95
Gems for the Young Folks (Juvenile Instructor Office)	7.95
Gems of Reminiscence (George C. Lambert)	12.95
Heber C. Kimball's Journal (Heber C. Kimball)	9.95
Helpful Visions (Juvenile Instructor Office)	7.95
Jacob Hamblin (James A. Little)	11.95
Labors in the Vineyard (Juvenile Instructor Office)	7.95
Leaves from My Journal (Wilford Woodruff)	11.95
Leaves from My Journal Study Guide (Woodruff/Monnett)	14.95
Life of Nephi, The (George Q. Cannon)	10.95
My First Mission (George Q. Cannon)	8.95
Precious Memories (George C. Lambert)	7.95
Scraps of Biography (Tanner, Tyler, Whitney)	9.95
Spaulding Manuscript, The (Reynolds/Spaulding)	14.95
String of Pearls, A (George Q. Cannon, ed.)	9.95
Treasures In Heaven (George C. Lambert)	7.95

November 23, 2016

NON-LDS BOOKS

Abraham Lincoln (Wilbur F. Gordy)	15.95
Alfred the Great (Jacob Abbott)	13.95
America's Founding Documents	5.95
Apocryphal New Testament, The	16.95
Bach: The Boy from Thuringia (Opal Wheeler & Sybil Deucher)	9.95
Benedict Arnold, A Biography (George Canning Hill)	17.95
Benjamin Franklin, A Biography (George Canning Hill)	19.95
Book of Enoch, The	12.95
Book of Jasher, The	15.95
Children of History, The (Mary S. Hancock)	13.95
Franklin: The Apprentice Boy (Jacob Abbott)	11.95
Heidi (Johanna Spyri)	19.95
High Uinta, A Novel (Robert D. Hatch)	14.95
Inspiration a Day, An (Rhanda Hunter Todd)	17.95
Island Story, An Vol. 1&2 (H.E. Marshall)	24.95
Israel Putnam, A Biography, General (George Canning Hill)	15.95
Life of General Lafayette (Unknown)	13.95
Mother of Washington (Nancy Turner & Sidney Gunn)	16.95
Mount Vernon: A Letter to the Children of America (Susan Cooper)	6.95
Nursery, The Vol. 1	12.95
Nursery, The Vol. 2	12.95
Our Home, Vol. 1&2 (C.E. Sargent)	21.95
Pilgrim's Progress (John Bunyan)	19.95
Play It Book, Days of Games for Children, The (Jean Fretwell)	10.95
Raising A New Generation of Patriots (Paterson, Hulse, Fletcher)	8.95
Revolutionary Adventures of Ebenezer Fox, The (Ebenezer Fox)	15.95
Stories of American Explorers and Settlers (Heard & King)	15.95
Story Hour, The (Kate Douglas Wiggin & Nora A. Smith)	12.95
This Blessed Land (Lezlee Jones)	15.95
War of Independence, The (John Fiske)	13.95

Archive Publishers
754 East 50 North
Heber City, UT 84032

www.archivepublishers.com
email: dan@archivepublishers.com
(435) 654-0824   Fax: (435) 654-4289

February 26, 2016